GW00372020

Tragedy and Social Evolution

Also by Eva Figes:

NOVELS
Equinox (Secker & Warburg)
Winter Journey (Faber & Faber, winner of the 1967 Guardian Fiction Prize)
Konek Landing (Faber & Faber)
B (Faber & Faber)
Days (Faber & Faber)

NON-FICTION
Patriarchal Attitudes (Faber & Faber)

FOR CHILDREN
The Banger (André Deutsch)
Scribble Sam (André Deutsch)

Tragedy and Social Evolution

Eva Figes

John Calder
LONDON

First published in Great Britain 1976
by John Calder (Publishers) Ltd
18 Brewer Street, London W1R 4AS
© Eva Figes 1976

ALL RIGHTS RESERVED

ISBN 0 7145 3516 8 Casebound

No part of this publication may be reproduced, stored in a retrieval system, or transmitted in any form, by any means, electronic, mechanical, photocopying, recording or otherwise except brief extracts for the purpose of review, without the prior permission of the copyright owner and the publisher.
Any paperback edition of this book whether published simultaneously with, or subsequent to, the casebound edition is sold subject to the condition that it shall not, by way of trade, be lent, resold, hired out or otherwise disposed of without the publisher's consent, in any form of binding or cover other than that in which it is published.

The author wishes to thank the Arts Council and the Phoenix Trust for financial assistance during the writing of this book.

In each case the translation of Greek plays is that used by the Penguin Classic Series.

Typeset in 11 point Times by Gloucester Typesetting Co Ltd.
Printed in Great Britain by Thomson Litho Ltd.,
East Kilbride, Scotland.

Contents

INTRODUCTION

Like other people, writers tend to look back to some fictional Golden Age when their professional situation would not have appeared quite so difficult as it now seems to be—a time when they were listened to, respected, and knew what they had to say; a time when they were materially rewarded according to their deserts and did not have to ingratiate themselves with anyone, or make compromises in order to succeed. People in all walks of life have a tendency to see the present as a falling away from the past, and to hark back to an imagined period when it was not so difficult to be a family man, housewife, worker, as it is now. They pick their scapegoats according to their religion, be it Marxism or middle-class morality.

I doubt whether it has ever been easy to be anything, let alone to write. However, individual genius is not necessarily enough, and it is important to be born at the right time. There have undoubtedly been periods of very special artistic achievement which can only be accounted for in historical and sociological terms. A tree, however healthy, will not bear fruit unless the soil and weather are right.

What does a writer need to succeed? Firstly, a language which is generally understood and which is rich, not only in vocabulary but in allusion, a language which is capable of bearing meaning: depending on the time and place you are born in, you may have to fashion your own meanings, or inherit a ready-made tradition which enables you to communicate much more easily and quickly to a large audience. Secondly, access to a medium of communication, if one exists at all. If you are born lucky you will choose or gain access to the dominant medium of the moment, if there is a choice to be made, and become a nineteenth-century novelist or a sixteenth-century dramatist; if you are born unlucky you may not have access to any medium of communication because you are born into the wrong class at the wrong time, or your religion is unorthodox. If, for instance, you were born into the working class, or a woman, earlier than the nineteenth century in England, there would have been no access of communication open to you—in any case, you would probably never have learnt to read or write.

Universal literacy and cheap printing are a very new phenomenon. Private enterprise, both on the part of scribblers and publishers, has allowed more and more people to become writers, and opened up the field of communication to people who would once have been excluded. Impossible to imagine a working-class poet opening up a subscription list in the eighteenth century, or a lady turning up, scripts in hand, at the sixteenth-century Globe. Indeed, it is doubtful whether even nineteenth-century publishers would have been broadminded enough to accept the first offerings of Charlotte Brontë or George Eliot if these ladies had not been protected by the anonymity of the Post Office and a male pseudonym. Media which require a higher degree of group consensus than book publishing—such as theatre and film—still tend to exclude women at a conceptual level, as writers and directors.

The novel tends to be a private act, both in the writing and the reading. As a result (provided always that a financial backer can be found) it allows for more diversity of expression, but the impact or 'success' of a novel is also more difficult to measure. Not only does the reading of a novel take place in private, it can tend to become associated with the privacy of the individual self, whether it be intimate thoughts or secret fantasies, and therefore become dissociated from what is apprehended as the 'real' world. In so far as the nineteenth-century woman of good family lived in a world of romantic make-believe which compensated for the boring restrictions of her real life, the reading of romantic novels fed those fantasies; in so far as twentieth-century man feels alienated, reading Kafka or Beckett will confirm his sense of alienation. But these readings belong to a private world, to our private thoughts. Once the book is closed we go back to our conventional behaviour and no one is any the wiser: the young girl put on her corset and made a sensible marriage; alienated man arrives at the office on time and answers his correspondence.

The theatre is different, being a public place. When we go to a play we are part of a large group in the auditorium. If we are shocked or moved by what takes place we are liable to feel exposed or vulnerable: we furtively try to remove the wetness from our eyes, or cover our unease by light conversation in the interval. But something has happened, and we are usually aware that it has not happened only to ourselves. We can become aware of the group reaction in a number of ways: in enthusiastic applause, in loud laughter, or in a tense stillness. At another level 'success' can be measured by the fact that there is not an empty seat in the auditorium and people are queuing at the box office. At both levels we become aware of participating in an occasion.

Drama thus has a very special impact, and theatre in a pre-literate society, or one that is predominantly illiterate, obviously has a particularly important function as a medium, not only to entertain but to instruct. But how did it get there in the first place? 'There can be no society,' wrote Durkheim, in *Elementary Forms of the Religious Life* 'which does not feel the need of upholding and reaffirming at regular intervals the collective sentiments and the collective ideas which make its unity and its personality'. Drama festivals held—as in ancient Greece or medieval Europe—at special times of the cyclic year, are an important means of reaffirming the collective ideas of a society. Scattered communities and groups are brought together to witness and participate in a vision of reality to which the audience basically subscribes, the only point of debate is how well that vision has been recreated. Groups, whether guilds or tribes, can compete with each other in trying to offer the best re-enactment, and the audience can vote on the best representation either directly, as they did in Athens, or by indirect means. In any case, the approval or disapproval of a social group is always important in drama: society may fragment into factions, as it has done in twentieth-century Europe, where many tastes and shades of opinion are catered for, but no dramatist can survive as a complete loner—he not only needs some sort of audience, but the group consensus of a theatrical company.

Most creative writers today tend to think of themselves as outsiders, writing against the consensus of their own society, or writing in the absence of any consensus at all. As a result many see the cure for their alienation in a new political structure, even though the history of the arts in totalitarian structures has not been promising. And yet some sort of totality seems called for.

I have chosen to write about tragedy because at certain times in history this literary form has represented a peak of artistic achievement which also looks like a totality. Distance makes it possible to take a more detached view. Why was it possible, in fifth-century Athens or sixteenth-century England, to produce works of such stature and content that men have tried in vain to emulate them ever since? I believe that to find the answer we must stray far beyond the bounds of conventional literary criticism, even beyond the bounds of 'historical background' as it is usually understood.

Poets as different as Milton and Shelley have looked back to tragedy as peaks of literary excellence. Milton defended tragedy 'as it was antiently compos'd' against the objections of Puritans by calling it 'the gravest, moralest and most profitable of all other Poems', which may not endear it to us but was high praise from him. The quotation comes from his introduction to *Samson Agonistes*, which is an attempt to emulate the Greek form. Two centuries later Shelley, in *A Defence of Poetry*, took a less obviously moral and more Durkheimian view when he called poets 'the unacknowledged legislators of the world' and maintained that 'the highest perfection of human society has ever corresponded with the highest dramatic excellence'. Like his contemporaries, Shelley tried to revive tragedy in the Shakespearian rather than the classical mode, but with equal lack of theatrical success.

Shelley's second statement, though it reveals a vague awareness of some sort of interaction between theatre and life, is obviously absurd. Elizabethan society was in many ways cruel and barbarous, and Shelley could hardly have approved of slavery or the disenfranchisement of women, both of which characterized Athenian democracy. So we have to look further afield for our explanation.

The origin of the word 'tragedy' is thought to lie in the Greek word for a goat, and though the ritual associations are obscure one inevitably thinks of the Israelite scapegoat, which Aaron was required to send into the wilderness with the sins of the community on its back. The rituals of cleansing and atonement did in fact require two goats, the second one being sacrificed for a sin-offering. We know that animal sacrifices were made at the start of drama festivals in Athens, as at other important public gatherings, such as the political assembly.

All primitive societies believe that human suffering is the result of human wrongdoing, whether deliberate or accidental, and that this intentional or unintentional sin must be expiated for good fortune to return. It is a concept which is still firmly embedded in the religions of societies which cannot by any means be called primitive. Christians have for centuries practised rituals of cleansing and atonement which imply the need to propitiate a vengeful higher power.

The more helpless human beings are in the face of a hostile environment, the more they need to believe that they can control that environment by their own conduct—by not sinning, and by assuming that personal or communal disaster can be averted or mitigated or driven away by ritual action. If they did not have such beliefs life would become unbearable, and men would see themselves as the helpless victims of circumstance, of weather, disease and death. Our own advanced civilization has tended to dispense with God and make man responsible for himself because we feel sufficiently in control of our own environment. When things go wrong our sense of outrage is appeased by laying the finger of blame on a human authority, whether it is the government or a doctor who made a wrong diagnosis. The finger of blame may be pointed with rationality, but if no obvious scapegoat or explanation can be found, if the malaise or disaster is large enough and apparently inexplicable, enlightened societies are quick enough to find an irrational scapegoat—such as a social minority, whether Jews, blacks, or communists.

In a primitive society, to appease the gods or spirits who have been angered, and to avert further disaster, a cleansing ritual has to take place. A person stricken by disease may have to ask himself what offences he has committed to deserve such punishment; alternatively, who bears him malice and is practising witchcraft. At a really primitive tribal level, human beings do not recognize death from natural causes at all, and all who die are the victims of witchcraft. This calls for revenge, to appease the angry spirit of the dead, particularly if the victim was important. In modern society the cleansing ritual takes the form of a committee of enquiry, or an autopsy. Disease and death become more acceptable if we can put scientific names to them: in this way we hope to avert them in the future by finding a cure.

Tragedy in the theatre is the sad story of a central protagonist who, either deliberately or by accident, offends against the most fundamental laws of his society, those laws which are so basic as to be considered divine. The divinity of the laws of a society are also related to human helplessness, to the inability of a society to see the laws enforced by any other means. A community which has little hope of detecting murder or theft, for example, for lack of an adequate police force, must rely on a communal belief in the all-seeing eye of God, and in supernatural powers which will both discover and punish an offender. In tragedy a community can see this process at work: the central protagonist who has polluted his environment, bringing disruption on himself and the community within which he lives, is eliminated, whereupon peace and order are restored. Whether that protagonist intended to break the divine social laws or not is beside the point.

Freud coined the term 'Oedipus complex' for his own purposes and has helped to foster the illusion that the stage Oedipus had a subconscious desire to make love to his mother. As a result of his influence we have tended to see Greek and indeed Shakespearian drama in terms of character and personal, subconscious motivation, rather than in terms of the total structure of the play situation. Not only have we had Hamlet without the Prince of Denmark, we have also had Hamlet as Oedipus. We have ignored the simple but telling precept of Aristotle, that it is action, not character, which matters in tragedy, because it is by our actions that we are rendered happy or unhappy.

The modern artist in Western societies tends to put a high value on originality, but in a society where theatre plays a central function in giving expression to and perpetuating the beliefs and ideologies of that society, the dramatist's originality is not of prime concern; he is often simply reworking traditional or familiar material, and if he is praised as a maker it is for the skilful way he projects that material, revitalizing it, rather than for originality of thought. For Greek audiences the stories of Oedipus and Electra held no surprises; they must have seen many representations of the same myths, and they judged a dramatist for his presentation, not his plot.

Ritual involves repetition; it also involves re-enactment. Whilst ritual re-enactment is intended to have magical properties which merely theatrical re-enactment does not, the latter is nevertheless important as a way of reinforcing belief and restating collective ideas. Both beliefs and social identity tend to be based on a mythological past which may or may not have some basis in fact, and re-enactment is often concerned with that past. Ritual re-enactment (as in Holy Communion, for example, which re-enacts the Last Supper) is intended to unify past and present in order to influence present and future, and tends to involve a cyclic view of history; dramatic re-enactment makes no such claim, but nevertheless has an important part to play in supporting political or religious beliefs. When small children at primary school perform nativity plays at Christmas they have no claim to a sacerdotal function, but the activity is undoubtedly intended to foster Christian beliefs in their impressionable young minds in a way which is much more real than mere story-telling. The past becomes a reality to actors and audience.

Today we still repeat ourselves to express collective ideas in dramatic form, but it takes different guises. Religious history has taken a back seat, and even secular history does not seem to be worked over by the entertainment media in a very significant way, though we can all think of exceptions, periods or personages who seem to have a perennial appeal to dramatists and film-makers, and whose actions are reinterpreted in the light of current beliefs or preoccupations. But the borderline between history and mythology is not easy to find, and much of what we regard as Greek mythology was once taken as history. The same is of course true of the Bible. If we think of the area of most repetition in modern drama for mass entertainment—in which we must obviously include cinema and television—we can see that there are stories which are repeated over and over again, though the protagonists may have slightly different names. The most obvious example in capitalist countries is the western. The American film industry mythologized the conquest of America by white Europeans in a way which has changed subtly over the past decades but obviously has a fundamental appeal far beyond the boundaries of the United States. The imperialist slant with racist genocide has gone, but the myth remains as potent as ever: urban man, hemmed in by restrictions and regulations, dreams of the wide-open spaces and aspires to the simple virtues of courage and initiative on which he fondly believes his present-day society to be based. The need for a rule of law is recognized but remains minimal (one sheriff), and private enterprise is checked only when it impinges on the freedom of others.

The idealized fantasy of the wide-open spaces is balanced by another myth, which lulls our anxieties as the other feeds our dreams. The second recurring drama is that of the police force with a tough, sympathetic police detective who always catches the offender. As our cities become more violent we have an ever-growing need to believe in an infallible police force. Police cars howl like the Furies after their man, whilst the detective combines paternal attributes with superhuman powers of deduction, and has an infinite amount of time to spare on a single unsolved crime. This bears little relationship to the realities of police work, but it is very reassuring. Murder will out, was the cry in Aeschylus and Shakespeare, who relied on a belief in an all-seeing power, in supernatural spirits. We do the same, for our own protection, though we give them different names. The path of retribution is laid with clues instead of portents, and a forensic expert may be called in instead of a seer, but the intention is much the same.

Although we tend to think of history as an academic subject it is fundamental to the way a society views itself: the selection and interpretation of facts, the simplified fable form which is taught to young children, and the equally fabled form in which it appears in our arts and entertainments. It is easier for us to understand this in relation to religion, since we live in a post-religious society which has rejected the histories of the Bible as mere stories, myths which reflect certain values; it is not so easy to see it in terms of secular history, although we have a whole publishing industry devoted to interpreting the past in terms of a Marxist millennium, rather as Shakespeare and his contemporaries interpreted past history as a vehicle for the culmination of Tudor glory, or theological writers have interpreted a variety of different events as heralding a Christian millennium.

We tend to distinguish between history and myth, fact and fiction, when it comes to civilizations far removed from our own. We have tended to dismiss the subjects of Homer's poetry and the dramas of Sophocles as mere stories, perhaps *because* they were treated in literary and poetic form, which we regard as separate from the study of history. And yet why should a society devote so much time and effort to redramatizing the same story year after year if it was not regarded as more than a story, as history embodying some important truth, even if, by the time Aristotle wrote, he had himself come to regard tragedies as based on silly stories? 'The subject of Greek drama,' wrote Gilbert Murray,

> is always the heroic saga. It is never an invented story, and it is never the history of ordinary human beings. I should doubt if there was any named character in an Attic tragedy

> who was not actually in some way an object of worship: a god or hero or at least the possessor of some taboo tomb or oracle or ritual.[1]

Normally, wrote Murray, the play portrayed some traditional story which was treated as the origin of some existing religious practice. Like nativity plays, or the many dramatic presentations that were once a feature of the Christian year.

Shakespeare used history books as his main source material, and in some cases, as for instance *King Lear*, used themes which had been dramatized before. One could say that this was a convenient way of providing a theatrical production at speed, but it would be more pertinent to assume that, if a historical theme was worked over more than once, it must have been considered to be particularly significant. It is also important to remember that the distinction between history plays and the tragedies is one made by us in the light of more accurate knowledge. Gorboduc, Lear and Macbeth are all listed by Holinshed, who also links the history of Britain with Biblical and classical 'history'. Britain, according to Holinshed, was originally populated by one of the sons of Noah; later it was invaded by Albion, son of Neptune, and Albion was killed by Hercules. Even *Troilus and Cressida* would have had a historical significance, at least in theory, to contemporary audiences, since the Tudor monarchy claimed a mythical Trojan ancestor who had come to rule Britain.

History represents precedence, which in turn represents natural justice. There is no better credential for a monarch, no more unifying symbol for his subjects, than a long and eminent ancestry. Most societies trace their beginnings back to a king or leader who was not merely royal, but had divine blood in his veins, and could claim the special blessing and protection of higher powers. History not only explains the rightness of things, justifies the occupation of a territory, the wielding of power, but is also used to explain the loss of power or happiness. The story of the Garden of Eden has many variations in many societies, and in patriarchal societies the fall from grace is invariably blamed on the woman, which explains her humble position since.

If *Macbeth* with its procession of future kings, its supernatural prophecies, can justify the establishment of a Stuart monarch, James I, on the English throne, through his mythical ancestor Banquo, the tragedy of *Richard II* explains the long historical turmoil which followed, and which was also dramatized. Perhaps Lear, as an ancient British king, was seen as one author and example of a divided kingdom which had caused so much bloodshed over so many centuries. Holinshed in the Preface to the *Chronicles* visualizes a golden age when Britain was under one ruler and, as in Eden-type myths, it came to an end through human sin:

> Well how soever it came first to be inhabited, likely it is that at first the whole Isle was under one Prince and Governor, though afterwards, and long peradventure before the Romans set foot within it, the monarchy thereof was broken, even when the multitude of the inhabitants grew to be great, and ambition entered amongst them, which hath brought so many good policies and states to ruin and decay.

Athenian drama festivals were preceded by ritual sacrifices, and the religious element was never really forgotten. Elizabethan secular drama filled a vacuum left after the abolition of religious dramatic festivals banned after the Reformation, but by focusing on a monarchy with divine pretensions it also satisfied a deep need.

This book attempts to explain some of the forces at work which contributed to unique peaks of artistic achievement. Many writers have tried to explain the power of great tragedy in terms of a 'moral order', which suggests a simplistic orthodoxy or an imposed didacticism, neither of which make for exciting art. The moral order is certainly there, but it consists of a complex network of beliefs and superstitions, images and associations, many of which may not be fully comprehended by either author or audience. This network belongs to certain times and certain places in history, and cannot be repeated; in order to understand some of the forces at work we have to explore some curious by-ways, as well as highways, and venture, however foolhardily, into disciplines far removed from the study of literary texts. In the process I hope that any reader curious enough to bear with me to the end will discover unexpected illuminations, not only about familiar and well-loved plays, but about human society and the human mind.

1 Tribal Drama and Belief

Towards the end of the nineteenth century two Victorian gentlemen called Baldwin Spencer and Frank Gillen spent the greater part of their adult lives making detailed studies of Australian aborigine tribes. They had a feeling of urgency, which they expressed in their written work, because they knew that the arrival of the white man would soon make it impossible to study these people at all. The aborigines faced imminent extinction. Already their way of life was being changed.

Anthropology was a new study at that time, and one which held a strong fascination for nineteenth-century intellectuals. The life of savages, wrote Freud, 'must have a peculiar interest for us if we are right in seeing in it a well-preserved picture of an early stage of our development', and for the study of social evolution it is the only picture we have. Freud, however, was struck by what he read as a parallel between the behaviour of 'savages' and the infantile conduct of neurotics, and here we are on decidedly dubious ground.[1]

The tribes that Spencer and Gillen studied were certainly savage by any Western yardstick. They lived in Central Australia, wore no clothes, occupied the roughest lean-tos made of shrubs, hunted for food, practised no agriculture, and were totemic in their beliefs and social organization. But the social behaviour which caused Durkheim, in *Elementary Forms of the Religious Life*, to draw on the work of Spencer and Gillen, was their habit of holding ceremonies which sometimes went on not just for days, but for months. Neighbouring groups would meet specifically for this purpose.

Before describing some of these ceremonies and considering their function it is necessary to say something about the social organization and beliefs of these people. I have chosen the studies of Spencer and Gillen not only because they give us such a clear picture of tribal ceremonies, but because many of the beliefs held by those tribes will be found in the drama of much more developed societies, in a residual form.

The natives had a complex classificatory system of relationships, which varied somewhat from tribe to tribe, and which governed marital relationships. Spencer and Gillen found that in one tribe group marriage was still practised. They believed that the practice in other tribes, whereby one particular group from one moiety of the tribe could only marry into one group of the other moiety, was also a leftover from previous group marriage. Freud, who read the work of Spencer and Gillen, believed that the savage had a quite peculiar horror of incest, and thus restricted his sexual activity to one eighth or twelfth of the tribe. Spencer and Gillen, who are mercifully sparing with broad generalizations, nevertheless make it quite clear that incest taboos have much to do with social organization and nothing whatsoever to do with the fear of fucking one's own mother or sister. However, most people's understanding of Oedipus is more conditioned by acquaintance with Freud's work than with the work of these or subsequent anthropologists.

In some tribes the totem to which a person belonged also governed the choice of a marriage partner, whilst in other tribes it did not. Totemism certainly played a part in the tribes' social organization, a complex classificatory system of kinship which we find so difficult to grasp because our own is based on different rules. But totemism was much more than that: it told the natives who they were, and why. It was history. Each man and woman was descended from a mythical ancestor, half animal, half human, an ancestor who had strange and divine powers which have since been lost to humanity. The landscape in which these tribes lived was not featureless at all: the mythical stories of totemic ancestors had taken place within it, and the natives knew exactly what episode had happened where. A tree there, a cluster of boulders here, they had acquired meaning and sacredness because of totemic history, and it was not dead history, but living and contemporaneous, because it affected what happened now. Just as, for Christians, the historic passion of Christ is also contemporaneous, made so by ritual.

The men of a particular totem were responsible for its continued supply, whether the totem was witchetty grub or emu, kangaroo or rain. Without these things the whole tribe would die. The old men knew the local totem spots, and passed on the knowledge from generation to generation, together with a knowledge of the ceremonies. They knew where an ancestor had stopped and left spirit children, where his body had died, going into the ground, leaving his spirit in the *churinga*, or sacred stones. A rock or tree now marked the spot.

Most of the totems were connected with food and many of the ceremonies were designed to ensure its continued supply. But among the Warramunga our anthropologists found the Wollunqua, a gigantic mythic snake which had to be propitiated in a series of ceremonies during which its history was enacted. Its wanderings marked out a tribal landscape, as did the history of the other totems:

> A few days after the series of ceremonies was completed we went off, in company with a little party of older natives, including the two headmen of the group, to visit Thapauerlu, the great centre of the Wollunqua totem. For the first two days our way lay across miserable plain country covered with poor scrub, with here and there low ranges rising. Every prominent feature of any kind was associated with some tradition of their past. A range some five miles away from Tennant Creek arose to mark the path traversed by the great ancestor of the Pittongu (bat) totem. Several miles further on a solitary upstanding column of rock represented an opossum man who rested here, looking about the country, and left spirit children behind him; a low range of remarkably white quartzite hills indicated a large number

> of white ant eggs thrown here in the Wingara* by the Munga-munga women as they passed across the country. A solitary flat-topped hill arose to mark the spot where the Wongana (crow) ancestor paused for some time, trying to pierce his nose; and on the second night we camped by the side of a water-hole where the same crow lived for some time in the Wingara, and where there are now plenty of crow-spirit children. All the time, as we travelled, the old men were talking amongst themselves about the natural features associated in tradition with these and other totemic ancestors of the tribe, and pointing them out to us.[2]

These men, of course, had no written history, they had never been to school, and yet they had a tribal history which was both detailed and vivid, and closely associated with the land in which they lived. At the end of this particular journey they took Spencer and Gillen to a waterhole under which the Wollunqua was supposed to live. At this point in the proceedings they became unusually quiet, bowed their heads, and addressed the Wollunqua in whispers.

In the valley below were heaps of rounded stones, carefully hidden behind boulders. The young men rubbed themselves with the stones, which represented a type of kangaroo called euro. They did this so as to be able to catch euro. The old men sang over the stones, rubbed them with euro fat and red ochre so that the supply of euro would continue to emanate from them. The cairns, they said, were very old: their fathers and grandfathers used to come and visit them, to rub them with red ochre and renew their bed of leaves. The larger ones represented old males, the medium ones the old female animals, and the small ones young euros.

The landscape of these tribes of Central Australia was imbued with a legendary history, mapped out with meaningful associations. Some spots had become shrines. The stories were perpetuated and kept alive by dramatic performances, ceremonies which not only served to keep the stories within the mem-

* *The dim and mythic past.*

ory of the social group, to pass them on to the new generation, but controlled present and future through a process of renewal.

There can be no doubt about the importance of dramatic ritual for these native tribes, an importance which is emphasized by the contrast between the elementary nature of their living conditions and the amount of careful and concentrated effort which went into the ceremonies. Firstly, the ceremonies obviously required a high degree of social organization, indeed, to some extent ritual and ceremony were central to the social cohesion of such a people, without written laws, without chiefs. They spent hours preparing themselves for the ceremonies, decorating each others' bodies with ochre and down to produce traditional patterns on their dark skins. The many photographs in the old volumes of Spencer and Gillen show just how much careful and painstaking effort went into the preparations.

For ceremonies connected with a particular totem, only initiated men were allowed to take part, whether as actors or audience. Even when a legend concerned a female ancestress the performer was male. Here is a detailed account of one of the ceremonies witnessed by Spencer and Gillen:

> The first performance was connected with the Unchalka grub of a place called Adnuringa, and as usual, during the preparation of the ceremony, no one was allowed to be present except the members of the totem. The upper part of the performer's body was decorated with lines of white and red down, and a shield was ornamented with a number of larger and smaller series of concentric circles of down. The former, according to the natives, represented the Unchalka bush on which the grub lives first of all, and the latter the Udniringa bush, on which the adult insect lays its eggs. This shield is spoken of as *churinga alkurta*.
>
> When the decoration of the shield and performers was complete, the men in the camp were called up and seated themselves on the ground in silence, forming a semicircle in front of the performer, who alternately bent his body double upon the ground and lifted himself up on his knees; as he did so he quivered his extended arms, which were supposed

> to represent the wings of the insect. Every now and again he bent forward, swaying up and down and from side to side over the shield, in imitation of the insect hovering over the bushes on which it lays its eggs. As soon as this ceremony was over the audience arose and silently walked across to the spot at which the performer of the second [ceremony] sat on the ground with two decorated shields beside him. He represented a celebrated ancestor of the Udniringita (witchetty grub) totem called Urangara. Of the two shields, a smaller one was ornamented with zigzag lines of white pipe-clay which were supposed to indicate the tracks of the Udniringita grub, while a bigger one was covered with larger and smaller series of concentric circles of down, the former representing the seeds of the Eremophila bush on which the grub feeds, and the latter the eggs of the adult insect. As in the first ceremony the men sat down silently while the performer wriggled, imitating the fluttering of the insect when first it leaves its chrysalis case in the ground and attempts to fly. There was no singing or dancing about, and when all was over the men sat for some time in silence, and then, as they gathered more closely together, the larger shield was taken and pressed in turn against the stomach of each of them.[3]

Such sacred performances arouse tensions which have to be relieved in some way. In Athenian drama the high tension of tragedy was given release in comedy. In Japanese Noh theatre the highly ritualized movements of the serious drama are followed by the irreverent tumblings of a comic sketch. Laughter is the release of tension. Aborigine drama also aroused tensions which required release:

> This touching of the body with some sacred object used during the performance of a ceremony is a very characteristic feature of all sacred ceremonies in the Arunta tribe. It is called *atnitta ulpailima*, which means, literally, softening the stomach. The natives say that their inward parts get tied up in knots, owing to the emotions which they experience

> when witnessing the ceremonies concerned with their dead ancestors, and that the only way to soften and untie them is to touch them with some sacred object . . .[4]

But it is not enough simply to consider the ritual drama of these people, one also has to know something about their beliefs and way of life. Ritual was not an isolated phenomenon, confined to the recreation of totemic or tribal history: their whole lives were imbued with it. Without ritual there would have been no social structure at all.

Some of the tribes ate their dead. Others buried their dead in the trees and, after a year or two, when the flesh had rotted away, disposed of the bones with final ceremonies. The bones were buried, the skull smashed. One arm bone was brought back to the camp and, after elaborate ceremonies and much wailing, also smashed, to indicate that the period of protracted mourning was over and that the spirit had gone back to its totem in the Wingara, the ancestral dream time, to await reincarnation.

Both men and women were accorded tree burial, since spirits alternated their sex with each incarnation. Sometimes a body was put straight into the ground if the dead person was extremely old, since the spirit was already enfeebled before death. But they never gave tree burial to a young man who had violated tribal law by taking a wife who was forbidden to him. Such an individual was called an *iturka*, a word which represented the foulest form of abuse in the language.

The widow, or widows, of the dead man were under severe restraint during the period of mourning, because his spirit was watching them. Later they would become the property of a younger brother. Their heads were shaved, their bodies smeared with ashes or clay. If this were not done to a widow the spirit of the dead man, who constantly followed her about, would kill her. Failing this, the younger brother could punish her by thrashing or even killing her. Until the final mourning ceremonies were over, a strict ban of silence was placed on the women of the deceased who stood in the relation of wife, mother, sister, daughter or mother-in-law, whether the relationship was actual or tribal. 'Amongst the Warramunga, especially, it is no uncommon thing to find that the greatest number of women in any camp are prohibited from speaking',[5] wrote our authors.

For these natives there was no such thing as death from natural causes: every death was attributed to somebody, and had to be avenged by another death. Spencer and Gillen witnessed one avenging party setting out. They returned several weeks later: having been unable to track down the culprit, who made his escape, they killed the guilty man's father instead.

The place where a man had died was smoothed down so that the tracks of the guilty party would show up. A snake track would indicate a man from the snake totem, for example. But, following a death, everyone immediately decamped from the vicinity, because nobody was anxious to meet the spirit of the dead man, or the spirit of the person who had caused the death by evil magic, who would probably visit the place in the form of an animal. The tree in which the corpse had been placed, wrapped up in bark and branches, was also visited, to find out whether the murderer had left any tracks. The male relatives would creep stealthily up to the tree to try and surprise the guilty spirit. Self-inflicted wounds were an obligatory part of the mourning rituals.

> The spirit of the dead person, called *ungwulan*, hovers about the tree, and at times visits the camp, watching if it be that of a man, to see that the widows are mourning properly; occasionally also it can be heard making a low kind of whistling sound. When the brother thinks it is getting near to the time for the final ceremonies he goes to the tree, and, addressing the spirit, says, 'Shall I go away?' If the latter says 'Yes,' he goes back to his camp at once, knowing that the time for the ceremony has not yet come. It is only after several such questionings that the spirit tells the man that it wishes the period of mourning to come to an end.[6]

These tribes accorded a particular reverence to their older men, who held the secrets of the totem and passed them down to the next generation. Secrecy was in itself a source of power.

A young man who had only recently been initiated could not expect to take part in all the ceremonies, to see, for instance, the hidden shrines of sacred stones and wood, the churinga which contained the spirits of the ancestors, and from which their present needs were supplied. Women and children had to avoid them altogether. The women, who in theory had only a vague notion where these storehouses were, always had to make a wide detour to avoid the area. The punishment for breaking this prohibition could be death.

If a man became so old and feeble that he could no longer perform ceremonies, some of the respect usually accorded might go, but normally a breach of the respect due to the authority of age was not tolerated. 'On one occasion,' wrote Spencer and Gillen,

> during a general quarrel, we saw one of the younger men, though he was, it must be remembered, quite mature and probably between thirty-five and forty years of age, attempt to strike one of the older men. The culprit was a medicine man, but, immediately, his medical powers departed from him.[7]

We have to go back to folklore to find the remnants of our own respect for the old. In fairy tales kindness to an old man or woman is still rewarded, unkindness punished, usually by supernatural or magical means. The curse or blessing of an old crone has power. It was also felt to have power at the time when harmless old women were executed for witchcraft. One powerful motive for exterminating them must have been the subconscious guilt of those who had lacked charity to the old and poor. No doubt the old woman who came begging to the door did utter curses if she was turned away empty-handed, and these were remembered when things went wrong in the household.

Until the time of Shakespeare the old also have a special place in high drama. In comic relief old men may appear ridiculous, as Aristophanes showed them, but in tragedy, which embodies all the highest aspirations and attitudes of a social group, old men must be respected. Often they are seers. Their wisdom must be listened to, their authority upheld, or ruinous disorder follows and society—seen as nature itself—is shaken to its foundations.

Amongst certain tribes group marriage still existed, in modified form, whilst in others, according to Spencer and Gillen, 'the terms of relationship indicate, without doubt, its former existence'. Whether or not Spencer and Gillen were correct in their interpretation, the marital customs they recorded must interest us for other reasons. For instance: 'Each tribe has one term applied indiscriminately by the man to the woman or women whom he actually marries and to all the women whom he might lawfully marry'.[8] The same applied in the case of his actual mother, and all the women his father might lawfully have married: 'A man, for example, will call his actual mother "Mia" but, at the same time, he will apply the term not only to other grown women, but to a little girl child, provided they all belong to the same group.'

If one transfers the story of Oedipus to a tribal society such as the one we have been describing it is no longer an outside chance or rare coincidence, one that can only be put down to Fate, to imagine that a man who has been brought up in a strange place, with no knowledge of the social group from which he came, might come back to kill his father and marry his mother. In a tribal sense it is quite probable. The chances against his marrying the right woman, and thus avoiding the disgrace of becoming an *iturka*, are seven to one against, since only one group out of eight is open to him. The dice of Fate are indeed loaded against him. Spencer and Gillen stressed that a man who broke the strict marriage laws was not merely afraid of punishment by a 'supreme being' or 'higher power'; he could, if found guilty, be put to death by his fellow men.

Marriages were usually arranged by the respective fathers or brothers of the couple. In a patriarchal society women have little say when it comes to the choice of a future husband, and women become a form of barter and exchange between men. In a patriarchal society the dramatic rituals which form such an important cohesive force in the community also tend to be a male preserve. Women are not totally excluded, but any ritual in which they are allowed to participate tends to be of secondary importance; usually they are only allowed to be the audience, and much of the ritual is intended to impress them and hold them in awe, and some rituals they are not even allowed to see.

Amongst the tribes studied by Spencer and Gillen boys when initiated, which involved elaborate rites, left the camp of women and children for good to join the men. Initiation involved being let into the secrets of the totem, being instructed in a very strict moral code, and being given to understand that any infringement of that code would be punished by the senior men. The boy also learnt that the spirit creature whom, up to that time, he had regarded as all-powerful, was merely a myth, an invention of the men to frighten women and children, so as to keep them obedient. The churinga, or bull-roarer, was given to the initiated youth, and he was told that he must on no account show it to the women and children, who believed that the sound produced by swinging it was that of a spirit.

For these tribes the mystique of ritual involved a hierarchy of authority, of senior men over their juniors, and of all men over women. As has already been said, the storehouses of sacred churinga were taboo territory to the women, who were not even supposed to know of their existence; women were excluded from the elaborate totemic ritual dramas, even as audience, where men would impersonate women if the mythology required it.

Ritual drama, where a sacerdotal function is involved, usually requires certain qualifications from those who take part: sex, seniority, and perhaps a hereditary lineage. Although the participators function on behalf of a wider community they also exert power and authority, in a society where ritual power may be the only kind available to deal with certain situations, and where the message they perpetuate and mediate cannot perhaps exist in any other form.

2 Kingship

We have seen that ritual drama, even at the most elementary level, involves the idea of history, and that history represents one form of collective identity. Whether that history has any basis in fact is irrelevant so long as the community has some belief in it; indeed, since the history which embodies the collective identity usually has to do with the supposed origins of that community, the establishment of its socio-political organization and its religious customs, the subject matter is very likely to be remote and mythological. One could almost say that it is difficult to imagine a collective identity at all without a sense of history, of something having once happened. Most religions are based on it.

The tribes studied by Spencer and Gillen were acephalous, and focused their dramas on the history and origins of their individual totems. When society has some kind of head, a leader, it is appropriate to concentrate dramatic action on such a man. When social organization includes some kind of kingship the king becomes a very obvious protagonist, because a king is at once an individual who acts and is more than a mere person. He is a very suitable figure to express the collective identity of a society because of the beliefs which are associated with kingship.

We can take peoples as widely separated in place and time as the Shilluk studied by Evans-Pritchard, Anglo-Saxon England and the Greece of Homer and find certain beliefs about kingship occurring again and again. In her book *Primitive Government* Lucy Mair points out that it is characteristic of peoples who recognize kingship to cherish myths which link its origin with some crucial event in their past history, not necessarily the creation of the world itself, but that 'his appearance is somehow linked with the establishment of the political order under which his subjects live'. In England, during the sixteenth century, the establishment of a new dynasty appears to have necessitated the invention of a new mythology, the Tudor myth. If Tudor mythology preoccupied both historians and poets to such an extent it can perhaps be explained by the break with the Church of Rome, so that the monarchy filled a vacuum and became the focal point of a new national cult.

But in societies which recognize kingship the king is not only a political head, he also has divine attributes. Often he can trace his ancestry to a god, which makes him a suitable mediator between his people and the higher power, and he usually has a ritual and sacerdotal function. The tombs of kings are often holy shrines.

The king, once chosen and installed, is held to embody in his person the welfare of the nation, and so he is often obliged to observe ritual precautions, the neglect of which would endanger his whole people. The ritual is usually most pronounced at the time of accession, when he may be anointed, when sacrifices may be made, and when he acquires the mystical power which comes with kingship. After the rituals of accession the personal rituals of kings were largely a matter of keeping their bodies pure and healthy, since their bodies were supposed to mirror the state of the nation as a whole. Sometimes their feet were not allowed to touch the ground. It is also assumed that many kings were not allowed to die naturally, since the dwindling powers of old age were seen as a dwindling of the life force, and in the case of a king his life force represented that of the nation. When a Nyakyusa king was dying his councillors stopped up the orifices of his body so that his soul should not escape, taking the fertility of the land with it.

Such a figure is obviously suitable for a drama which embodies the central belief of a community. And we do not have far to look. The story of kings was so central to Greek drama that the *skene* represented the façade of a palace, and if Frances Yates's conjecture is correct (see her *Theatre of the World*) Shakespeare's stage also represented the front of a castle or palace.

We know that tragedy usually involved a 'change from prosperity to adversity', as Aristotle put it, though for Aristotle the only reason for having a king as the protagonist was the fact that he had fortune and prosperity to lose. And yet we know that the welfare of a king involved the welfare of his people, so his misfortune or misconduct would appear to explain the misfortune of his people. Indeed, in the story of Oedipus this is made quite explicit, since it is the incestuous behaviour of their king which has brought a plague to the people of Thebes.

An inadequate king must be got rid of and replaced for the benefit of the people. Most tragedies end with the death of the protagonist and his replacement by a new leader. Not only African communities were in the habit of disposing of weak or ailing kings. 'The most fundamental concept in Germanic kingship,' writes William Chaney in *The Cult of Kingship in Anglo-Saxon England*, 'is the indissolubility of its religious and political functions. The king is above all the intermediary between his people and the gods, the charismatic embodiment of the "luck" of the folk.' When the king's luck ran out and he could no longer secure the divine blessings, the people were justified in replacing him by a more effective ruler. A king's effectiveness depended in large part on surplus wealth, and this wealth came from the people. When times were hard, when crops failed, for instance, the king lacked wealth with which to buy loyalty and entertain his followers, which weakened his effectiveness. Appropriately the Anglo-Saxon words for 'lucky' (*eadig* and *saelig*) were also used to mean 'rich'. Burgundian kings under whom crops or victory failed were deposed, and when bad harvests continued in Sweden in spite of the ruler's sacrifices, he was killed. His successor was equally unlucky, and was burnt in his house as an offering. We are not so far from Homer's famous passage

> When a blameless and god-fearing king maintains impartial justice the brown earth is rich in corn and barley, and the trees are laden with fruit; the ewes constantly bring forth young, the sea abounds in fishes; nothing that does not prosper when there is good government, and the people are happy (*Odyssey* XIX. 109).

This passage clearly reveals the magical qualities associated with kingship during Homeric times, since we know that—however just and pious a king may be—he cannot control the weather. It was a period when clan and tribal chiefs could trace their ancestry to the gods, and the king of the city, the king of kings, was he whose divine origin was most incontestably established, his function being first and foremost that of high priest, a mediator between gods and men. Similarly, all the royal houses of the Anglo-Saxons for whom genealogies remain claimed divine descent, mostly from Woden, and later the pagan genealogies were assimilated to Christianity, so that the mythical lineage of King Aethelwulf of Wessex, for instance, was traced back through Woden, who was in turn descended from a son of Noah. A large proportion of Anglo-Saxon saints belonged to royal families and their burial places also became sacred shrines. 'If the leaders do not serve God,' wrote Aelfric in one of his homilies, 'God will manifest to them their contempt of Him either by famine or by pestilence'; and as a purifier of his people the king continued to exercise his divine power by touching for the 'king's evil' for centuries to come, until well after Shakespeare's lifetime.

Not only do these facts throw a very different light on the famous story of King Canute and the waves, they force us to ask whether there is, fundamentally, all that much difference between portraying the life and passion of Jesus Christ, the Son of God but also the Son of Man, who suffered and died so that man might be saved and purified from sin, and the suffering and death of a king who claims descent from Zeus, Apollo or Nyikang, the leader of the Shilluk in their heroic age. Of course the human attributes, the stresses and difficulties of living in a real world, receive a greater emphasis when the chief protagonist is an earthly king: after all, even Agamemnon was only the great-grandson of Zeus, and all the kings in drama are human enough not to have deliberately pre-rigged their fate in advance. And yet some of the same elements are there: the fundamental tie between a king and his people, and the need for a purge or purification which will release his people from suffering. The most obvious example is the story of Oedipus, who breaks fundamental social taboos which literally brings a plague on the city of Thebes, but the central concept can be successfully adapted to a more secular view of kingship, involving a more modern view of *Realpolitik*. For instance, Evans-Pritchard took a more practical view of the killing of an ailing king than the usual one of a direct link between the body politic and the royal body:

> The assertion that a sick or old king should be killed probably means that when some disaster falls upon the Shilluk nation the tensions inherent in its political structure become manifest in the attribution of the distaster to his failing powers. The unpopularity which national misfortune brings on a king enables a prince to raise rebellion.[1]

And it is obvious that when a king is 'weak', whether physically or morally, factional strife becomes more likely. 'Strong' government is associated with the peace and prosperity of a nation. The dilemma of the weak king who must be eliminated but who is nevertheless sacred, and the troubles this brings upon his people, is amply explored by Shakespeare. In the figure of Lear weakness is associated with age, in Richard II it is associated with youth.

The most obvious and immediate objection to this line of thought so far as Greek tragedy is concerned is the fact that fifth-century Athens had abandoned traditional kingship and had a system of government far removed from Homeric feudalism. However, quite apart from the fact that the works of Homer remained a kind of Bible, some curious vestiges of kingship remained. The magistrate or archon who held the title of king had a sacerdotal function, and his wife had to be a virgin on marriage. She was required to go through an annual rite representing her marriage and corporal union with Dionysus. In the king archon's hands, wrote Aristotle, were all the ancestral observances, and Plato wrote that 'to him who has obtained the office of King have been assigned the most solemn and peculiarly ancestral of the ancient observances'.

Thus we see that the king's most important function, the sacerdotal one, was still very much alive in fifth-century Greece (and many societies which recognize kingship do not have a rigid hereditary system, but go through the process of choosing a new king). Other oddities reminiscent of traditional kingship survived: elected archons did not take up their duties until they had been examined on their ancestry by the council, the process known as *dokimasia*; furthermore, the archons were to have no physical defect,[2] a requirement which is typical of a sacred kingship, and which seems contrary to both democracy and rationalism.

Having understood that physical defects still disqualified a man from holding high office in fifth-century Athens, we are confronted with the story of Oedipus yet again. Oedipus means Swollen-foot, a name given to the infant child by his rescuer: when his parents left him to die they riveted his ankles. Oedipus did not need to kill his father and marry his mother to disqualify himself for his high office (and we have already shown that in a tribal situation no intricate 'web of Fate' so beloved of critics, would have been necessary for him to do that)—his physical deformity was an *a priori* disqualification. We do not know whether contemporary performances made his disability obvious, but to Greek audiences the name must have been revealing enough.

So how did Oedipus come to hold his high office? He was of course a *tyrannus* and not a hereditary monarch, and from what we know about kingship patterns, both in Greece and elsewhere, it is safe to assume that he became tyrannus by marrying the widow of his predecessor. There is an interesting suggestion, put forward by Frazer in his *Early History of Kingship*, that matrilineal descent may have persisted longer in royal families. There are innumerable examples in Greek mythology: Menelaus, for example, went to Sparta, married Helen, and reigned there; his brother Agamemnon reigned in the land of his wife Clytemnestra, and their father Atreus had migrated from Pisa to rule in Mycenae. His father, Pelops, had also migrated to succeed his father-in-law on the throne. (The bitterness of Electra, married off to a peasant after her father's murder takes on a new dimension.) Other Greek families followed a similar pattern of inheritance, notably the relatives and ancestors of Achilles.

Now according to Saxo Grammaticus this was also the custom in Denmark. (We begin to get a new understanding of the many fairy tales about wandering adventurers winning the hand of a princess and thus a kingdom.) A man could certainly acquire the kingdom by marrying the widow of his precedessor, even if this involved killing the previous king. Hamlet's uncle Feng came to the throne in this way, as did Hamlet's successor, Wiglet. In Lydia, according to Herodotus, Gyges murdered the king and reigned over the country by marrying his widow; and this was not the only instance of such a succession in the history of Lydia. 'The tame submission of the people to their rule,' wrote Frazer, 'would be intelligible, if they regarded the assassins, in spite of their crimes, as the lawful occupants of the throne by reason of their marriage to the widowed queen.' It would also, of course, stop her leading a rebellion, and make the claims of the murdered king's descendants more difficult. Such considerations of *Realpolitik* must have been behind the wooing of the machiavellian Richard III. We are not told why Oedipus married Jocasta, or why Claudius married Gertrude, but since both women must have been well into middle age, and old by any but twentieth-century standards, one must assume that both Claudius and Oedipus were motivated by a lust for power rather than sexual passion.

Much has been made by past critics of the curious 'blindness' of Oedipus in failing to examine the pattern of events which brought him to power as represented in the play by Sophocles. Post-Freudian analysis has tended to suggest that Oedipus deliberately suppressed certain facts from his conscious mind because, presumably, of his Oedipal longings. But this is stretching credulity too far. Are we really to believe that Oedipus, after being married to the widowed queen for several years, long enough for her to have children by him, never heard from Jocasta the circumstances of his predecessor's death? Are we also to assume that the people of Thebes held no enquiry into the killing of their leader, and did not try to seek out the offender? Surely not. But the curious situation becomes explicable if, in earlier versions of the Oedipus story (and there must have been many) Oedipus deliberately killed Laius and married Jocasta to become tyrannus, and his marriage was sufficient to validate his position in the eyes of the Thebans. It is probable that in an earlier version the pollution which Oedipus brought upon the city was through his unwitting parricide and incestuous marriage (which may, going even further back in the story's origins, have been incestuous merely in a tribal sense) without the further complication of his being ignorant of the circumstances surrounding the murder of his predecessor on the throne.

This last complication could have been a late addition to the story, to explain an otherwise inexplicable situation to a patriarchal democracy which no longer practised matrilineal descent through the royal family, and no longer understood it. Frazer believed that the various reasons assigned by Greek writers for the migration of princes, a common one being banishment for murder, was an attempt to explain a matrilineal system, which was no longer practised and understood. The fact that Homer has Oedipus continuing to reign, although pursued by the Erinyes, after the discovery of the murder of Laius, may be a clue to such an earlier version of the myth.

The idea of a Freudian 'Oedipal' situation in either *Oedipus Tyrannus* or *Hamlet*, with a marriage motivated by sexual passion rather than power, becomes even more absurd when we understand just how widespread a custom marriage by a new king to the dead king's widow (even if she was his stepmother) once was. The custom existed in England, and amongst the Warni and other Continental tribes. Canute married the widow of his predecessor, Ethelred, whose children he had driven into exile, even though she was much older than him and was anyhow living in Normandy. Eadbald of Kent married his stepmother when he came to the throne after the death of his father

Aethelbert, and Judith, queen of the ninth-century Aethelwulf of Wessex, was married to his son and successor when the old king was dead.

The link between Hamlet and Oedipus, and more particularly between Hamlet and Orestes, is one of situation based on what would appear to have been universal kingship patterns in societies which acknowledged kingship. The quite peculiar problem of Oedipus is that he is both Claudius and Hamlet, and must therefore inflict punishment on himself. If Hamlet's relationship to his mother is different from that of Orestes, it is because she was not an accomplice in the murder of his father, so Hamlet can only reproach her for her indecently hasty remarriage, which he ascribes to lust in someone old enough to know better. But Gertrude is hardly a very amorous character; instead she is fearful, torn between anxiety for the son she loves and a politic marriage. This is a situation which a contemporary audience, used to politic marriages, particularly in their royal families, would have understood. Hamlet's dilemma is to know whether the ghost is a genuine and benign manifestation, whilst Orestes has to fulfil one obligation (revenge) and in doing so break a fundamental taboo by killing his mother. But their situation is similar in that both come back from abroad to a powerful *fait accompli*, and both adopt disguises of one sort or another to achieve their mission.

The sacerdotal function of the king is particularly emphasized in Greek drama, both within the play and in the way which drama festivals were themselves conducted, as part of a religious festival which included ritual sacrifice of animals. Agamemnon first addresses himself to the gods on his return from Troy in the trilogy of Aeschylus, which immediately establishes him as a 'good' king as far as his people and the actual audience are concerned. We know that he once went so far as to sacrifice his own daughter, which is the main cause of Clytemnestra's bitterness, but we are not asked to pass judgment on this action, except to see it as a cause for conflict. In a country which made a regular practice of exposing unwanted children, particularly girls, the contemporary judgment would no doubt have been in favour of Agamemnon, who was only carrying out his public duty in order to obtain victory at Troy, whilst Clytemnestra was merely allowing womanly and private emotions to cloud the issue—that Aeschylus was heavily patriarchal is not in doubt anyhow.

Oedipus, as portrayed by Sophocles, assures his stricken and distressed people at the beginning of the play that he will carry out all the necessary rites. His assurances betray a certain anxiety not only because his people are suffering, and he may be blamed for it, but because he was a tyrannus, who ruled like a king but could not claim divine descent like hereditary kings. As a result these rulers followed a policy of religious observance designed to win them the trust of the people and compensate for their lack of an ancestry which could guarantee protection. Instead they had to ingratiate themselves with the gods and thus, to some extent, with the people.

The king fulfils a priestly function, but he is human as well as divine. The actor in playing the king fulfils a priestly function, in playing the role; the king who is the king is also playing the role, since he has at some time in his life been chosen to play the part, and after his departure someone else will fill the role.

Since a king embodies the luck of his people certain taboos are usually connected with his body and his daily conduct. His feet must not touch the ground, or he must not eat certain foods; polluted murderers must not come near him. In societies which have developed a more sophisticated philosophy of the monarchy, as in Shakespeare's England, the king is seen more as someone who should set a good moral example to his people, but the physical link between God-king-people is far from lost. Princes, wrote Antonio de Guevara in the book translated by Thomas North as *The Diall of Princes*, should be better Christians than their subjects, firstly because they have to set a good example, and secondly because they will be punished in the hereafter not only for their own sins, but for those of their subjects whom they led astray: 'For if a fountaine be infected, it is unpossible for the streames (the issue thereof) to be pure.' Princes, he declared, would also have to 'render accompt of their estates' to God, rather like stewards.

In a less sophisticated society, one with less control over its own good or ill-fortune, the king's responsibility is a good deal more direct than that. As we have seen, he could be killed for a failed harvest. It is significant that in the story of Oedipus his offences against the gods are only uncovered *after* the city of of Thebes is struck by plague. It is a basic pattern of the primitive, superstitious thought process, to look for a cause to explain personal or collective misfortune. If the cause is not maleficent witchcraft it must be the anger of gods or spirits at some sin, wittingly or unwittingly committed. One must pacify this anger by sacrifice. By creating an imaginative machinery of cause and effect, in this case dramatized in tragedy, the participants nurture the illusion of divine law, which is also divine justice, which controls the machinery which crushes them. However devastating the vision, it nevertheless creates the hope of avoiding ruin at some time in the future if the divine laws are observed.

When a blameless and god-fearing king maintains impartial justice, wrote Homer, the brown earth is rich in corn and barley, and the trees laden with fruit. In Seneca's *Oedipus* Creon, reporting the words of Laius's ghost, tells the people to expel Oedipus, which will not only get rid of the plague but make the grass grow green again and cause 'the beauty of the woods to bloom again'.

Lienhardt's study of the religion of the Dinka[3] affords us considerable insight into the pattern of belief in cause and effect, and the need for sacrificial action. 'It is true,' he wrote, 'that misfortune is associated by the Dinka with some offence; but often the seriousness of the offence is not known until the results then attributed to it have been experienced.' When, for instance, a man is sick, a diviner is called in to diagnose the sickness, and to discover 'a reason for the action of the power on the ailing man in some sin of omission or commission'. Once the grounds for the suffering are recognized symbolic action is taken in animal sacrifice: the power is said to be 'cut off' or 'separated' from the man, and his suffering placed upon the back of the sacrificial victim:

> Without these Powers or images . . . there would be for the Dinka no differentiation between experience of the self and

> of the world which acts upon it. Suffering, for example, would be merely 'lived' or endured. With the imaging of the grounds of suffering in a particular Power, the Dinka can grasp its nature intellectually in a way which satisfies them, and thus to some extent transcend and dominate it in this knowledge.

The system works satisfactorily because all human beings sin and they must all, at some time, suffer. It is therefore easy to correlate the two factors and conceptualize a kind of divine justice, however slowly the wheels of the divine machinery may creak forward. This is the pattern of tragic drama, which provides the audience with both a warning and with consolation, a spurious wisdom. The consolation is not only in the possibility of alternative patterns of action, but in the idea that the powers of mighty men are not absolute, but are in turn controlled by a higher power which acts as a regulator.

The actor who plays the king is playing a role—he is not directly fulfilling a sacerdotal function, but only providing an example for the audience to watch; the king who is a king is also playing a role, since his 'part' will at some time be taken over by someone else, and since he is made king by virtue of the drama of the coronation rituals, and the regalia which are his props. This duality can enrich the drama: Shakespeare makes use of it, when his Macbeth and Richard II display self-awareness of themselves as actors on a stage. They are of course actors in a double sense, and in this way all the world does become a stage, and the concept of theatre as a microcosm is reinforced.

At some stage in social evolution it is no longer tenable to burn the king when the crops fail. The correlation between the welfare of the people and the conduct of the king has to be seen in more subtle and less superstitious terms, and this is when the idea of the king as an example to his people takes over. Plato, who lists the qualities of a good king as being temperance, good memory, intelligence, courage and nobility of manner, took this view:

> a monarch, when he decides to change the moral habits of a State, needs no great efforts nor a vast length of time, but what he does need is to lead the way himself first along the desired path . . . by his personal example he should first trace out the right lines, giving praise and honour to these things, blame to those, and degrading the disobedient according to their several deeds (*Laws*, Bk IV).

What is surprising is that Plato should assume that it is easy for a monarch to change the morals of his subjects, and this is an assumption which is usually made by monarchists who think kings should rule by setting a good example. And Plato, of course, was not a monarchist anyway, which makes his statement even more surprising. It is still assumed that there is something special about kingship, as opposed to other forms of government. Sir Walter Ralegh, who was a staunch monarchist, also had a simplistic faith in the efficacy of a moral monarch. 'Subjects are made good by two means,' he wrote in *The Cabinet-Council*, 'by constraint of law, and the prince's example; for in all estates the people do imitate those conditions whereunto they see the prince inclined.'

Here there is a belief that people imitate examples set before them. Theatre is both an imitation and an example. Aristophanes believed that the necessity of a powerful moral example in the theatre was so strong that it required a poet of the stature of Aeschylus to 'save the city'. In *The Frogs* he prefers Aeschylus to Euripides because he is the better teacher, and likely to give better advice to his audience in a time of crisis.

That the king acts a part, and does not necessarily act it well, is expressed in Tasso's *The Householders Philosophie* which was, aptly enough, translated into English by the dramatist Kyd. Tasso draws a parallel with the theatre:

> whatsoever others say, thou art thus to understand, that this distinction of *Sovereign*, *Ruler*, *Governor*, or *Master*, is first founded upon Nature, for some are naturally born to command, and others to obey. And he that is born to obey,

> were he of the King's blood, is nevertheless a servant, though he be not so reputed; because the people that only have regard to exterior things judge none otherwise of the conditions of men than they do in Tragedies of him they call the King, who, apparelled in Purple and glistering all in Gold and precious stones, represents the person of *Agamemnon*, *Atreus*, or *Etheocles*; where if he chance to fail in action, comeliness, or utterance, they do not derogate from his old title, but they say *The King hath not played his part well.*

Life, says Tasso, is a 'Theatre of the world'. Some princes 'act' better than others. Machiavelli took the concept one step further when he took the idea of 'acting' as a form of dissimulation, not to inspire the people, but to hoodwink them.

Shakespeare's Richard II does not play his part well. He does not play it well in two senses, firstly because he does not have the attributes of wisdom, temperance and judgment which make for a good king, but also because he is so very conscious of playing a role—he is, let us face it, downright theatrical. He dramatizes himself, and insists on wringing the last vestiges of pathos and irony from any given situation. The audience, both on and off stage, are aware that he is playing a role, putting on an act. Bolingbroke loses patience with his self-dramatizing, his determination to make a big production number out of each situation. In a political sense, he does not act effectively at all.

Macbeth, on the other hand, is a real man of action. He starts as a hero, and if he had been born to play the part of king he would have made a good job of it. It is only at the very end of the play, when his wife is dead and he himself faces defeat and death, that he realizes that the whole bloody mess, his usurpation of the throne and the murders which followed it, were all not worth while, and that being a king merely involves playing a role for a little while. He need not have bothered, and his ambition was worse than wicked—merely futile.

The idea that the anointed king is merely playing a role, one which he may act well or badly, is also reflected in the concept of the king's two bodies, the 'body politic' and the 'body natural'. The 'body natural', wrote Edmund Plowden in his *Commentaries*, is 'subject to all the Infirmities that come by Nature or Accident, to the Imbecility of Infancy or old Age', but

> his Body politic is a Body that cannot be seen or handled, consisting of Policy and Government, and constituted for the Direction of the People, and the Management of the public-weal, and this Body is utterly void of Infancy, and old Age, and other natural Defects and Imbecilities which the Body natural is subject to, and for this Cause what the King does in his Body politic cannot be invalidated or frustrated by any Disability in his natural Body.

The body politic 'wipes away every Imperfection of the other with which it is consolidated'. So that 'he has a Body natural adorned and invested with the Estate and Dignity royal'. Like an actor.

During Shakespeare's lifetime a king was still required to be clean-living, not so much because of a primitive belief in pollution following the breaking of taboos, or rituals left undone, but because the king had to set an example. He not only had to do this so that his subjects would copy the example, but in order to govern wisely and well. 'A man must first govern himself,' wrote Ralegh, 'ere he be fit to govern a family; and his family, ere he be fit to bear a part in the government of the commonwealth.'[4] Ralegh recognized that royalty were subject to special temptations. 'Great princes,' he wrote, 'rarely resist their appetites, as for the most part private men can.'[5] He had no doubt that a bad king had to be endured as an unfortunate Act of God, 'as fire, floods and other inevitable plagues are necessarily to be suffered'. It is necessary for princes to resist their appetites and wherever possible to listen to those older and wiser than themselves. 'Experience hath proved that commonweals have prospered so long as good counsel did govern; but when favour, fear, or voluptuousness entered, those nations became disordered.' And he goes on to say that 'The election of counsellors is and ought to be chiefly among men of long experience and grave years'.

All of which inevitably reminds us of Richard II, who was governed by his appetites and jeered at the counsel of old John of Gaunt.

Thus the king's personal habits continued to have a special significance in spite of a more sophisticated view of politics and kingship than that encountered amongst ancient Germanic people or, more recently, African tribes. This gives a new dimension to the long eulogy to Henry V which we find in Holinshed's *Chronicles*, and enables us to understand why Shakespeare's Henry had to turn his back on his old cronies on becoming king. The eulogy is very long, and Henry is described as a 'captain against whom fortune never frowned', a just and courageous king, who left no offence unpunished, no friendship unrewarded. But most noticeable is the emphasis on the purity of his private life. 'This Henry was a king, whose life was immaculate, and his living without spot.' We are also told that 'he did continually abstain himself from lascivious living and blind avarice'. In *Macbeth*, when Malcolm tests Macduff by pretending that he would make an even worse king than Macbeth, the first sin he lays claim to is voluptuousness and unbounded lust, and the second is 'a staunchless avarice'.

The concept of kingship as a fountainhead of pure living and hence good government is most aptly expressed by Webster in *The Duchess of Malfi*:

In seeking to reduce both state and people
To a fix'd order, their judicious king
Begins at home: quits first his royal palace
Of flatt'ring sycophants, of dissolute
And infamous persons . . .
Consid'ring duly, that a prince's court
Is like a common fountain, whence should flow
Pure silver drops in general: but if't chance
Some curs'd example poison't near the head,
Death, and diseases through the whole land spread.

Plowden also described the king as the 'fountain' of all 'Justice, Tranquility and Repose', which for him justifies the royal prerogative, which puts the king above the law. As we have seen, Guevara also described a prince as a fountainhead, on which the purity of streams depended. Plowden also uses an image with which we are familiar through Shakespeare (particularly *Coriolanus*), that of the king as head of a body, 'the Members thereof are his Subjects, and he and his Subjects together compose the Corporation'.

As a result the business of the king is the business of everyone, which is a good justification for re-enacting his deeds on a public stage, so that everyone should know about them. Plowden wrote that 'every Subject has an Interest in the King, and none of his Subjects that is within his Law is divided from the King who is his Head and Sovereign. So that his Business and Things concern the whole Realm.' This view of the king is reflected in Holinshed's description of Henry V: 'Every honest person was permitted to come to him, sitting at his meal, and either sincerely or openly to declare his mind and intent.' The image of Henry keeping open house to his subjects is almost feudal in conception: the royal palace as a meeting place for subjects. Significantly, Holinshed also praises Henry for his liberality, in spite of his own immaculate living.

The plays written by Shakespeare and his contemporaries dealt with the history of past kings. It is quite clear, both from these texts, and from other literature, such as Ralegh's writing, that subjects had no right to rebel against an evil or inadequate king. They had to suffer the yoke, because of his divine position. This view of kingship goes back to Anglo-Saxon times. 'The people,' wrote Aelfric, 'have the option to choose him for king who is agreeable to them; but after that he has been hallowed as king he has power over the people, and they must not shake his yoke from their necks.' Shakespeare's Richard II relies on the fact that

Not all the waters in the rough rude sea
Can wash the balm of an anointed king

and in the long-term he is proved right, because the usurpers are ultimately punished, though not within his own lifetime.

But many of the plays deal with kings who were either downright evil, or injudicious, or voluptuous. How are we to explain this in the light of contemporary monarchist philosophy? Firstly the kings written about were all dead, and secondly history can provide 'examples' in more senses than one. History, wrote Ralegh in the Preface to his *History of the World*, allows us to see 'how kings and kingdoms have flourished and fallen; and for what virtue and piety God made prosperous, and for what vice and deformity he made wretched'. Holinshed saw the uses of history in similar terms. Whilst Montaigne gave *carte blanche* to critics of kings when he wrote:

> Let us make this concession to the political order: to suffer them patiently if they are unworthy, to conceal their vices, to abet them by commending their indifferent actions if their authority needs our support. But, our dealings over, it is not right to deny to justice and to our liberty the expression of our true feelings, and especially to deny good subjects the glory of having reverently and faithfully served a master whose imperfections were so well known to them, and thus to deprive posterity of such a useful example (BK I, *Essay 3*).

Dead kings no longer require our uncritical obedience; on the contrary, we owe it to ourselves and posterity to tell the truth, however unflattering to the dead monarch. The king is required to control his appetites, according to sixteenth-century political philosophy in England, not because of any automatic pollution, as would be the case in a less developed society, where the king's functions are primarily sacerdotal, and not only because the king provides an example for his people to follow, although this is important enough. A king who is ruled by his appetites cannot make just and rational decisions, and does not treat his subjects with fairness and impartiality. He also becomes subject to bad influences at court. This sounds highly idealistic but is more concerned with *Realpolitik*, since the subjects with whom a monarch must deal fairly are not the peasantry, who do not matter a damn, but the nobility, who can cause a great deal of trouble if they feel they have a grievance.

Both Edward II and Richard II were considered by Holinshed as inadequate for these kinds of reasons, and Marlowe and Shakespeare gave the examples living reality by dramatizing the dire consequences of such regal weakness. For Holinshed Edward II exemplifies the anger and discontent which is aroused amongst the powerful nobility if the king has a particular favourite. In his *Maxims of State* Ralegh used the famous Elizabethan concept of 'degree' to emphasize that a king must control his nobility by ensuring that honour, power and wealth are fairly distributed amongst them. (The common people are relatively unimportant—in *The Cabinet-Council* Ralegh writes that 'the vulgar sort is generally variable, rash, hardy, and void of judgment', which is very much the way Shakespeare portrayed them.) All historians and dramatists of the period warn against the dangers of flattery and bad advice, which can lead a monarch astray. In elaborating his concept of 'degree and due proportion', Ralegh wrote that it was important for the king to ensure that no nobleman should

> so excel in honour, power, or wealth, as that he resembles another king within the kingdom, as the house of Lancaster within this realm. To that end, not to load any with too much honour or preferment, because it is hard even for the best and worthiest men, to bear their greatness and high fortune temperately, as appeareth by infinite examples in all states.[6]

Here, in a nutshell, we have the tragic story of Macbeth, a valiant nobleman who was overloaded with honours by a king too weak to fight his own battles, and who could not bear his high fortune 'temperately'. Shakespeare does not emphasize the regal weaknesses of Duncan in his play, where the main emphasis is on his age, but Holinshed tells us that Duncan was 'soft and gentle of nature' and 'negligent in punishing offenders', so that his reign was upset by 'seditious commotions'. But the worthiness of Macbeth in the eyes of his fellow nobles and the king, and the latter's reliance on him, are never in doubt in the early, expository part of the play. Duncan had failed to keep political 'degree', and chaos came upon his kingdom as a result.

The seditious commotions which plagued Richard II were also of his own making, and thus provided a useful example for posterity. Unfortunately, in the case of Shakespeare's play on the subject, the historical example came uncomfortably close to reality: Elizabeth saw herself as Richard and the supporters of the rebellious Essex had the play revived in 1601 for propaganda purposes. Holinshed wrote that Richard

> forgot himself, and began to rule by will more than by reason, threatening death to each one that obeyed not his inordinate desires: by means whereof, the lords of the realm began to fear their own estates, being in danger of his furious outrage whom they took for a man destitute of sobriety and wisdom, and therefore could not like of him, that so abused his authority.

Thus Richard lacks the personal virtues of clean-living and temperance which were thought essential to good monarchy, and also fails to observe Ralegh's 'degree'. The fact that almost the entire nobility should have rallied to the Duke of Lancaster is emphasized by Holinshed as 'a very notable example, and not unworthy of all Princes to be well weighed'. Essex, however, proved no Bolingbroke.

Holinshed, in the preface to his *Chronicles*, stated his belief that the main purpose in the writing of history was 'the daunting of the vicious' by 'penal examples', apart from the encouragement of patriotism. If Richard II provided one penal example, no one more than Edward II illustrated the consequences of wanton living in a monarch. Through the influence of Gaveston, writes Holinshed,

> he was suddenly so corrupted, that he burst out into most heinous vices . . . he began to have his nobles in no regard, to set nothing by their instructions, and to take small heed unto the government of the common wealth, so that within a while, he gave himself to wantonness, passing his time in voluptuous pleasure, and riotous excess . . .

Piers Gaveston saw to it that Edward's court was full of 'jesters, ruffians, flattering parasites, musicians, and other vile and naughty ribalds', so that the king spent 'both days and night in jesting, playing, banqueting and in such other filthy and dishonourable exercises'. Moreover, he procured 'honourable offices' for these ruffians, and antagonized the peers of the realm by his arrogant manner.

If historians thought the main function of history was to provide political 'examples' of virtue rewarded and vice punished for the instruction of the living, there is no reason to suppose that the authors of historical plays did not see their function in a very similar light. The fact that vice can be so entertaining is of course an added bonus.

The chronicling and dramatization of the history of past kings serves to provide examples for the contemporary audience or reader. But another function is also served, and that is the justification and explication of the present. We have seen that such a function was served in Greek tragedy, where the stories dramatized helped to provide an origin and to explain a current religious rite or custom. A similar function is served by Christian nativity and passion plays, and the ritual drama of the aborigines also served to explain the present in terms of a dim and distant past, the Wingara.

The Shakespearian plays which deal with the real or supposed past of the British Isles also serve a purpose of this kind. The most obvious example, with which every student is familiar, is the whole series which (chronologically in history) follows on the tragedy of *Richard II*, through the civil turmoils which followed, to the establishment of the glorious Tudor present. But *Macbeth* is another example, although it is not usually seen in this light, since it is a self-contained play, set in a dim and distant past, a play which is both a highly entertaining thriller and constructed in a way which conforms neatly to the theories of Bradley or any other critic of the tragic 'form'.

Macbeth was written shortly after the accession of James VI of Scotland to the English throne. With his reign began a new dynasty, and we see this dynasty foretold in the play, by the witches who prophesy and reveal an unending line of kings descending from Banquo, the fictional ancestor of James I, first Stuart king of England. Shakespeare got Banquo from Holinshed, who got him from Boece, who invented both Banquo and the witches in order to give the Stuarts a respectable pedigree. No doubt James must have been pleased to see a play with so much emphasis on witchcraft, since he firmly believed in witches, but the long line of kings stretching to the crack of doom, ie. long past James himself, must have been even more gratifying.

In a society basically committed to the idea of a static state, prophecy is a way of validating political change. Thus the invention of Boece, visibly dramatized by Shakespeare, helped to make a new royal family acceptable to a public who had only recently been inculcated with Tudor mythology. Prophecy gives an added force to this long pedigree, because it is supernatural and therefore implies both inevitability and divine sanction. The fact that the witches are agents of the Devil (and their prophecies to Macbeth are deliberately misleading) is a theological point which Shakespeare rather glides over. In his *Daemonologie*, published in 1597, only a few years before his accession to the English throne and the composition of *Macbeth*, James VI of Scotland discussed at some length whether the Devil and his agents could look into the future, and concluded that although witches could make some guesses by judging from past experience and the laws of natural causes, true prophecy belonged to God. The theological dilemma can, however, be resolved by the assumption that a contemporary audience would have regarded the line of kings as 'true' since the Stuarts had already ascended the English throne, thus fulfilling the prophecy. If the witches were allowed to show the truth, no doubt it was only to punish and torment Macbeth.

We have already tried to show at some length that disaster as a punishment for sin is a concept of cause and effect inherent in tragic drama, as it is inherent in a religious view of the world. It pre-dates the scientific rationalism which has, since Shakespeare's day, overtaken our own society and changed our attitudes to most, though by no means all, misfortunes that can overtake mankind.

In the sixteenth century history and politics were very much viewed as part of such a pattern of cause and effect, and it was not only the poets who imposed that kind of order on reality and on the past.

One of the disasters which the Elizabethans feared most was civil war, and strong monarchy provided security against such dissension. The Wars of the Roses provided a recent example of the horrors such political chaos could bring upon a nation. 'The greatest and most grievous calamity that can come to any state is civil war,' wrote Ralegh. Such calamity is viewed as the result of sin, a punishment brought upon the people. In Shakespeare's famous history cycle the Wars of the Roses follow on the sin of regicide. Holinshed constantly ascribes foreign invasions to internal factions: the Romans, he writes, were able to invade Britain 'the sooner doubtless, by reason of the factions amongst the Princes of the land', and the Saxons were always quarrelling and fighting amongst themselves, 'so as no perfect order of government could be framed, nor the Kings grow to any great puissance, either to move wars abroad, or sufficiently to defend themselves against foreign forces at home'. Foreign invasions are punishments for misdemeanours at home (*Lear*, *Macbeth*, and *Hamlet* all end with a foreign invasion force). Insufferable tyranny, on the other hand, is also punished by the hand of God. The Danes, wrote Holinshed, were so barbarous that God

> would not suffer them to continue any while over us, but when he saw his time he removed their yoke, and gave us liberty, as it were to breath us, thereby to see whether this his sharp scourge could have moved us to repentance and amendment of our lewd and sinful lives, or not. But when no sign thereof appeared in our hearts, he called in another nation to vex us, I mean the Normans.

Holinshed believed that in a dim and distant golden age the whole island had been ruled by one prince, and that this idyllic state of affairs had been ruined by 'ambition' and internal strife.

Like all golden ages, it is seen as ending through human sin. It also reflects the wistful longings of a people who had been having trouble with the Welsh and Scottish peoples for many, many centuries.

Two plays of the period mirror this vision of unity and its destruction. Both are set in ancient Britain, and thus provide an origin for the afflictions which have beset the English people since those dim and distant times through human—and particularly royal—folly. One is *Gorboduc*, written by Thomas Norton and Thomas Sackville in 1561 and usually termed the first English tragedy, and the other is *King Lear*, written forty years later. Although we do not think of these plays as 'histories' we must remember that to contemporary audiences Gorboduc and Lear, just like Macbeth, were historical kings. All three figure in Holinshed, for example.

Both *Gorboduc* and *King Lear* feature an ancient king who, because of his advanced years, wishes to abrogate his responsibilities and divide his kingdom amongst his heirs. (The failing powers of an old king can here be linked in a very real way with a belief in kingship which inspires certain societies to equate the health of their king with the life force of the society itself, and thus dispose of an ailing king.) Lear divides his kingdom between two of his daughters, disinheriting the third, and Gorboduc divides his kingdom between his two sons. In each case the result is civil strife.

The play of *Gorboduc* starts with a dumbshow designed to signify that 'a state of unity doth continue strong against all force, but being divided, is easily destroyed', a sentiment very much in evidence in the writings of Holinshed. *Gorboduc* is a crude play but it is useful for a greater understanding of *King Lear*, because it overtly expresses many of the political concepts which are implicit in Shakespeare's play. It also helps us to understand how Shakespeare, using the theme of the abdicating king *and father*, fused the relationship between natural order and political order into a poetic whole. A link which is much more baldly stated in *Gorboduc*.

Gorboduc, like Lear, is deaf to wise counsel when he first makes his decision to abdicate. In most societies age confers higher status on a man, but in societies which are conceived of as inherently static, that is, governed by a natural order which is also the political order, which exists for all time and is divine in origin, age and seniority confer special status which must be observed. Seniority was strictly observed amongst the aborigine tribes we have been looking at; age was also linked to status in fifth-century Athens. Thus, by allowing himself to be ruled by his own children, Gorboduc (like Lear) is overturning the natural order, which is also the political order. One of his advisers warns him

To yield to them your royal governance,
To be above them only in the name
Of father, not in kingly state also,
I think not good for you, for them, nor us.

And the reason why it is not good for either the royal household or the country at large is spelt out:

Nature hath her order and her course,
Which (being broken) doth corrupt the state
Of mind and things, ev'n in the best of all.

Much has been written about the concept of 'nature' in *King Lear*. In Shakespeare's play the emphasis is on the 'unnatural' behaviour of children, and from there the whole play is broadened out into a dialectic on what should be regarded as natural and unnatural. What is not brought out in the text itself is the fact that Lear was himself behaving in an unnatural way by abrogating his responsibility as king and father, and that by abdicating his authority he was himself the author of the chaos that followed. Of course we see, as a twentieth-century audience, that he was to blame in that his behaviour was rash, autocratic and foolhardy, and we may regard him as an unnatural father in his behaviour to Cordelia. But a contemporary audience would have understood, without having to be told, that his real irresponsibility lay in abdicating and dividing the kingdom. In Shakespeare's plays fathers are habitually authoritarian in their dealings with their daughters: this in itself would not have seemed blameworthy to Shakespeare (who obviously had troubled dealings with his own daughters) or to his patriarchal audience.

A man, said Ralegh, must first learn to govern his own family before he is fit to govern the commonwealth, and before that he must learn to govern himself. Lear obviously cannot govern himself, and when he gives up his kingdom he also gives up the ability to govern his family. Gorboduc is warned of the consequences of his action

> *When fathers cease to know that they should rule,*
> *The children cease to know they should obey;*

We must remember that in a society where age is an element in the structure of social hierarchy, the necessity for 'children' to obey and respect their elders, particularly their parents, most particularly the father, does not cease when they become adults. The sons of Gorboduc are obviously not minors, or there could be no question of dividing the kingdom between them. In Shakespeare's *King Lear* we have both a questioning dialectic on the nature of Nature and a much more subtle characterization because Shakespeare understands that such a hierarchy of seniority raises problems: his daughters are grown-up women with minds of their own, just as Edmund is no less a human being for being born a bastard. And as Cordelia rightly points out, once a woman marries half her love and duty must go to her husband, who is her new lord and master in the patriarchal system.

Gorboduc, which is a relatively crude play devoid of real poetic imagination, reads more like a political tract in places. As a result it provides useful information on contemporary attitudes, when a greater work, like *King Lear*, cannot necessarily be regarded as representative. The authors of *Gorboduc* also recognized that the hierarchy of age seniority raised real problems. In relation to the problems of primogeniture they discuss the sibling rivalry which can follow as a manifestation of the goddess Nature:

And such an equalness hath Nature made
Between the brethren of one father's seed,
As an unkindly wrong it seems to be,
To throw the brother subject under feet
Of him, whose peer he is by course of kind;
And Nature, that did make this equalness,
Oft so repineth at so great a wrong,
That oft she raiseth up a grudging grief
In younger brethren at the elder's state:
Whereby both towns and kingdoms have been rased,
And famous stocks of royal blood destroyed:

Edmund's famous monologue in *King Lear* is usually regarded as the last word in irreverence, but the above speech, which is spoken on good authority by a wise counsellor, would appear to give him some justification in contemporary eyes. If Edmund's attitude was not correct, it was at least understandable:

Thou, Nature, art my goddess; to thy law
My services are bound. Wherefore should I
Stand in the plague of custom, and permit
The curiosity of nations to deprive me,
For that I am some twelve or fourteen moonshines
Lag of a brother?

It is significant that his first objection is not to being discriminated against on the grounds of being a bastard, but because he is a year younger than his brother. So he appears to justify his attitude firstly by telling the audience that he intends to obey the goddess Nature, as is only natural, a concept that they were already familiar with (as *Gorboduc* shows) and strengthens his case by the complaint about being a younger son, before going on to argue against the concept of bastardy. No doubt there were many younger sons in the audience who were only too ready to sympathize. Both plays recognize that in some points Nature seems to be at odds with itself, and certainly at odds with human customs and the social order, and no doubt contemporary audiences understood this from personal experience. The basic philosophy of a social and political order based on 'natural' order was not always as neat in practice as it was made out to be in principle, and the dramatized conflicts as presented in the theatre could attempt to resolve them, not necessarily in argument, but in the ending of the play, which is the resolution. In the case of Edmund his argument is undermined by making him a metaphorical bastard, a thoroughly bad lot. His logic may be impeccable, but his actions turn the audience against him. When he goes under his original argument appears to have been refuted. The *status quo* is restored, the custom of primogeniture and legitimacy appears to have been justified, and the audience have long forgotten (if they were inclined to sympathize with Edmund) that he really would have appeared to have suffered a basic injustice in the first place. A modern dramatist, working within a different system of ethics, would present Edmund as socially deprived, someone with a chip on his shoulder as a result of emotional or economic deprivation in his formative years, a criminal as a result of a broken home, with an absentee father or mother.

Gorboduc gives us an origin for the loss of that golden age which Holinshed and his contemporaries envisaged, a time when Britain was ruled by one monarch, and its people enjoyed peace, since lost for ever. When Gorboduc is warned against dividing his kindgom one counsellor tells him

> *Within one land, one single rule is best:*
> *Divided reigns do make divided hearts;*

And he is also reminded that his ancestor, the mythical Brutus, made a similar mistake when he divided his kingdom between his three sons:

> *But how much British blood hath since been spilt,*
> *To join again the sunder'd unity!*

But Gorboduc does not follow 'grave advice', instead he

follows 'wilful will' and is a victim of flattery, thus showing very much the same weaknesses as Lear. At the end of the play the British people are left with no monarch at all and the threat of an imminent foreign invasion. The equation between civil strife and an inability to resist foreign invasion, so clearly stated in Holinshed, is also clearly stated in this play. The parallel with the ending of *King Lear* is also obvious. We are surely not making too great an assumption in thinking that a contemporary audience would have seen in Shakespeare's play yet another origin of later strife. At the very least he provided a warning and example. Like Gorboduc, who

A mirror shall become to princes all,
To learn to shun the cause of such a fall.

If Lear is at once an example of how kings should not behave and a possible origin for the British falling away from a supposed golden age of political unity, he is also something much more. In history he may be one of the first kings of the island, but in a poetic and imaginative sense Shakespeare sees him as the end of a line, the last of a line of kings. He did of course depart quite fundamentally from Holinshed, who had Lear restored to the throne by the forces of Cordelia, but also departed radically from an earlier dramatization of the story, which also ended happily. One could say that his pessimism was inspired by reading a little further into Holinshed, who tells us that Cordelia succeeded her father to the throne, but that her nephews levied war against her and took her prisoner, whereupon she killed herself. But the feeling one has that Lear is the last of a line of kings is reinforced by the perfunctory and ambiguous ending: the political order is not restored, no one really believes in Edgar as the next ruler, least of all himself. He is only a stand-in—for what? The answer is left blank, a vacuum is suggested. Instead of a moral and positive speech to round the play off we have four sad lines, the ambiguity of which has been commented on by Peter Brook in *The Empty Space*:

The weight of this sad time we must obey;
Speak what we feel, not what we ought to say.
The oldest hath borne most: we that are young
Shall never see so much, nor live so long.

To me the second line suggests a deliberate rejection of the political platitude of order restored, whilst the last two suggest that the time of chaos is not over, and that Edgar and his contemporaries will have short and violent lives, and cannot expect to die quietly in their beds of old age.

As an entity the play of *King Lear* presents us with a very profound exploration of the nature of Nature, and a dialectic on two opposing points of view runs right through it. Some characters, notably Edmund, present a cynical view of the universe where both human nature and the forces of nature are cruel, and where the gods do not care what happens to us, and even enjoy our sufferings. The other view, represented by the forces of right, maintains that the gods are just, and that wickedness will inevitably be punished in the end. Now, the first view undoubtedly comes over more forcibly throughout the play, and although Shakespeare makes his wicked characters die one feels that they did so more by accident than through any Grand Design. The positive view is put forward very feebly—by Albany, for instance, who hardly comes across as a strong character. Gloucester, who starts off as foolishly complacent in his religious beliefs, becomes highly pessimistic as a result of his suffering, and is only reconverted to piety by a trick in his pathetic blindness, one which is visible to the entire audience. Edgar may be doing him a kindness in deceiving him, but it is a kindness played upon an old man who cannot bear too much reality.

Now the position of kingship depends upon a belief in a natural and moral order which also includes a political order. Kings were put there by God, and their subjects' obedience depended on a recognition of this fact. One very practical reason for continued support for the monarchy in sixteenth-century England was this divine sanction. 'Monarchies royal,' wrote Ralegh in *The Cabinet-Council* 'are for the most part ancient and hereditary, and consequently easy to be governed. For it is sufficient for the prince to maintain the old laws, and on occasion temporise with those accidents that happen.' Machiavelli also recognized the practical advantages of hereditary rule.

But what if there is no such divine and natural order, no degree upon which the monarchy depends? In *Richard II* we are certainly shown that it is no good a monarch depending too heavily on his divine status, but nevertheless his actions and what happens to him are incorporated into that broader political philosophy of a bigger order embracing incidental chaos. This is not the case in *King Lear*.

Lear certainly breaks the rules of monarchy by being arrogant, wilful, and deaf to good advice. But Shakespeare's characters in this play do not argue a political case, as they do in *Richard II* or *Gorboduc*. Ultimately the struggle is not between human beings fighting for power but between Lear and the elements. Richard relies on the fact that he has been anointed by the society over which he rules, but Lear goes much further: he abandons political power but still relies on a special relationship with the gods (expressed in non-Christian terms as Lear is supposed to be an ancient British king). He is constantly calling on the powers above to pour curses on his disobedient daughters. When he disowns Cordelia he summons down Jove's thunder, and demands that lightning should strike her blind.

But the elements are indifferent to his regal authority. They do not, it appears, distinguish between a king and the meanest beggar. When the storm breaks, it is Lear who gets wet.

In a sense Lear has only himself to blame, as the Fool points out. In a society which equated old age with wisdom, he had grown old without growing wise and he had turned degree topsy-turvy, like Gorboduc, in making his daughters his mothers. But the vision of chaos and monstrosity which the play represents goes far beyond any sin of omission or commission on Lear's part. He has indeed spawned monsters, humanity does 'prey on itself', and Goneril and Regan are offsprings of the same legitimate marriage bed as Cordelia; they cannot be explained away, like Edmund, on the grounds of bastardy and an adulterous relationship.

Did Shakespeare see Lear as a 'last' king, the end of a line, in the sense that he represented a type of kingship no longer associated with his own period, the kind of kingship we find in tribal societies, or in Anglo-Saxon England, or was he doing a more thorough demolition job in associating him with kingship in general? It seems to me that the historical sense of Shakespeare and his contemporaries was very unlike our own, and such distinctions between different kinds of monarchy would have been quite alien to him. Sixteenth-century historians viewed the past as basically a static state, interrupted by periods of commotion from time to time, and their own period with its monarchy as a continuation of that static state. I think that one therefore must conclude that the vision of the universe which Shakespeare presented in *King Lear* was one which made the concept of kingship a nonsense and an absurdity. Lear is not deposed or usurped in the normal way of histories or historical tragedies. He is gradually made aware of his own humanity, his weak flesh, his affinity with the meanest beggars in the land once his royal trappings are stripped away. Calls to the powers above are useless, they are deaf and blind and the heavens merely piss on his unprotected head. He does not need to be got rid of by murder: he dies of his own accord, of a broken heart.

Shakespeare had done with history, and the tragedy of kings. From them on his kings belonged to fairy land, to romances where reconciliation between fathers and daughters, husbands and wives, was still possible; his kings belonged to a world of make-believe where wounds could still be healed and lost kingdoms restored. We may regard this as a higher wisdom, but there is no doubt that Shakespeare turned his back on monarchism as a positive political reality.

From then on the history of kings was to play an increasingly unimportant part in English drama. With the bourgeois revolution and the execution of Charles I the figures of kings lost their symbolic and political potency. The need for examples was lost, since bad kings could be disposed of and did not represent the organic head of the state. One could chop the head off and the state would survive. The taboo surrounding the awesome sin of regicide was lost, and the killing of the king no longer represented an explanation for consequent political turmoil or public and private suffering. The Restoration of 1660 did not bring with it a restoration of the old charisma surrounding the monarchy, and attempts at tragic drama set in royal palaces were a flop. Instead the theatre depicted a world of wealthy immorality and private pleasure, totally divorced from any sense of social responsibility.

In France the hothouse flowering of the French tragic drama of royalty represented an absolutism enforced by strict literary censorship. The tragedies of Corneille and Racine are written specifically for an élitist audience, and they represent all too clearly the divorce between monarchy and people. The royal personages in these dramas have no political responsibility, they move in a goldfish bowl of private passions, obsessed with honour, divorced from the rest of society. Ordinary mortals have no place in these plays except as servants, confidants conveniently placed to listen to their woes. Significantly, these dramatists could not draw on the real history of the French people and its monarchy; they were forced to draw on a false, neo-classical model and parade their characters in togas or Spanish costumes, anywhere, just so long as the setting and costume were not French. And if necessary classical models had to be altered so as not to offend the gratifying self-image that the French aristocracy had of itself, as quite unlike the rest of humanity. Strange as it may seem to us, with our theatrical traditions, Racine's characters were often considered scandalously unkinglike. Corneille was better at toeing the political line and giving his tiny public what they wanted. But even Racine altered the story of *Phèdre*, for example, so that it is her nurse who accuses Hippolyte and brings about his death—he thought such an action unsuitable for a princess. 'Cette bassesse m'a paru plus convenable a une nourrice, qui pouvoit avoir des inclinations plus serviles', he wrote.

French absolutism and censorship resulted in tragic drama which not only did not reflect the ideals and aspirations of a cross-section of society, a collective consciousness; it did not even reflect the true humanity of the tiny minority to whom it was addressed. What the drama does reveal is the extent of the divorce between rulers and ruled, the lack of any sense, so strong in English writing of the sixteenth-century, that the king's business is the business of everyone, because the welfare of the nation depends on him, and that his royal prerogative is dependent on his royal responsibility. Kings are not shown to govern, well or badly, and do not provide examples. Marooned in their palaces, their tragedies are purely private, honour and duty conflicting with passion and desire. No commotion, no fighting, no sounds of thunder breaking overhead. But in the silence, with hindsight, we can hear the tumbrils beginning to roll.

3 The Dead

Most of the tribes studied by Spencer and Gillen practised tree burial of their dead, followed some time later by burial of the bones in the ground. As in the story of Antigone and her two brothers, the burial ritual was a duty owed by the living relatives to the dead, but denial of proper burial was a dishonour deliberately heaped upon those who had themselves dishonoured the tribe: 'they do not bury in the trees any young man who has violated tribal law by taking as wife any woman who is forbidden to him; such an individual is always buried directly in the ground'.

The authors described the mourning ceremonies they witnessed amongst the Warramunga which, because of their protracted nature, must have occupied a considerable proportion of their lives. The spirits of the dead were feared, and had to be propitiated. The tree burial took place, but:

> Next morning there was not a sign of any habitation to be seen on the side of the creek on which the dead man's camp had formerly stood . . . Every camp was removed to a considerable distance from the scene as no one was anxious to meet with the spirit . . . of the dead man, which would be hovering about the spot, or with that of the man who had brought about the death by evil magic, as it would probably come to visit the place in the form of an animal.[1]

Our own folklore has many stories of murdered men and women whose spirits haunt their former homes, or the places where they died, but since these tribes did not recognize the concept of natural death, since for them every death was the result of evil magic performed by someone, the drama of propitiating the spirit took place after every death. This could only be done by finding the killer and killing him or her in turn. So the tree grave was regularly visited in the hopes of surprising the spirit of the murderer, as was the spot where the man had actually died. 'If for example, a snake track were visible, then this would be regarded as a sure sign that a man of the snake totem was the culprit.' The divination of the murderer by the medicine man was followed by an avenging party organized by the dead man's kin.

Avenging a person's death was the duty of male relatives, whilst protracted mourning was the proper duty of female relatives. If the dead person was a man, his spirit was liable to visit the camp to see that the widows were mourning properly. When a young man died amongst the Unmatjera and Kaitish tribes the younger brother, who would inherit the widow, shaved her head; she covered her body with ashes during the period of mourning. If this was not done the spirit of the dead man, who constantly followed her about, would kill her and strip all the flesh off her bones. In addition the younger brother would be justified in severely thrashing or even killing the widow, if he were to meet her, during the period of deep mourning, without this emblem of sadness. If he did so the action would no doubt help to propitiate his brother's spirit. Malinowski, in writing about the Trobrianders, emphasizes the social aspect of mortuary rituals. He writes that 'in the Trobriands there is not one single mortuary act, not one ceremony, which is not considered to be an obligation of the performer towards some of the other survivors', and he writes that the widow's grief 'affords direct satisfaction to the deceased man's brothers and maternal relatives'.[2] However, although this is no doubt an important aspect of mortuary rituals it must be considered secondary in societies which retain an active belief in spirits.

Seligman, writing about the Azande of the Nilotic Sudan,[3] said that they believed that, whatever the mode of death, the real cause was witchcraft, and that the dead man's spirit remained near the tomb until the duty of taking vengeance had been performed. Unlike the Australian aborigines, the Azande confined their vengeance to magic. When someone died the medicine man had to determine whether the vengeance was now complete. Roscoe records a similar attitude to death amongst the Baganda:

> Death from natural causes rarely presents itself to the native mind as a feasible explanation for the end of life; illness was much more likely to be the result of malice finding vent in magic art. . . . Any illness of the King was generally attributed to ghosts, because no human being would dare to practise magic upon him.[4]

The Baganda also believed that widows were liable to be watched over by their departed husbands: 'When a man wished to marry a widow, he first paid the deceased husband a bark-cloth and a fowl, which he put into the little shrine at the grave; in this way he imagined he could pacify the ghost.' And, as is usual in societies which have kingship, the mortuary ceremonies for a king had a particular significance. The king had a shrine built for his father, wrote Roscoe, where the medium came to give the oracles. In Anglo-Saxon England the tombs of many kings became shrines, as did those of ancient Greek kings.

Even if not all deaths require very positive action on the part of the living, spirits who have cause for grievance are very liable to haunt their living relatives until that grievance has been avenged or put right. Roscoe writes of the Baganda that: 'Relatives dreaded a member of their clan being put to death unjustly, because of the trouble the ghost was able to give them; hence they were willing to do all in their power to help him, even if they had no love for him.' Evans-Pritchard reports a similar attitude to the dead amongst the Nuer: 'Four to six months after the burial the mortuary ceremony is held. Its purpose is to wipe out the debt which the Nuer feel to be due on account of the death. The ghost of the dead has to be appeased or misfortune may come to the living.' The Nuer believe that a man haunts his kinsmen because he was killed and they neither avenged him nor exacted compensation in cattle for his death. A man who has not been properly buried may also haunt his kin. Evans-Pritchard writes:

> it is only those who have recently departed who avenge themselves on the living, for it is only they who can have been wronged by them . . . a dead man seems to be more dangerous . . . the less the lapse of time after his death, and consequently in the period between death and the mortuary ceremonies. Those nearest to the dead are those who are most likely to be affected . . . the closer the relationship of the persons concerned the worse both the offence and its consequences.[5]

If a man kills a close kinsman he loses his wits, sickens and dies. If he commits serious incest the aggrieved party, that is, his father, will haunt him when he dies.

The duty of kinsmen to avenge murdered relatives is so strong that it is one of the last duties to be taken over by some form of judicial system. 'It may be significant,' writes Lucy Mair, 'that revenge for murder was still left to the victim's kin to execute, even where courts of justice were as highly developed as they were in Buganda. No doubt the reason for this is the idea of vengeance as the last duty owed by kinsmen.'[6] And Schapera writes:

> Until some time after the middle of the nineteenth century the Hottentots practised blood vengeance. If a man was killed accidentally, his family might accept compensation in cattle. But if he was murdered or killed in a fight, his brother or son had to avenge him, even if the opportunity did not occur for many years. Neither chief nor council might intervene to prevent this, nor could they punish the avenger.[7]

In Anglo-Saxon England, as among all Germanic peoples, it was a fundamental convention that the killing of a free man brought his kin into immediate action in order to avenge his death, or to enforce the payment of his *wergild.* The slayer's kin were expected to pay the wergild or bear the feud that was the alternative.

Under Athenian law only individuals, not the state, could bring a suit. There were private suits, and public suits brought by any citizen who considered himself injured as a member of the public. But the crime of homicide, on account of the taint which was attached to the guilty man and which threatened to infect the whole city, always retained the character of an offence against the gods. Where homicide involves the need to mollify the spirit of the dead person it also involves the idea of pollution. Evans-Pritchard, for instance, records that amongst the Nuer a man who slays another may not drink until a priest has made sacrifice and cut his right arm. The kin of the slayer and the kin of the slain may not come in contact by eating or drinking from the same vessels until the blood-feud has been closed by a payment of cattle and by sacrifices; a third person could cause death by eating or drinking with both factions. In Anglo-Saxon England four laws—two of King Edmund and two of Aethelred the Redeless—forbad anyone polluted by homicide from approaching the king, unless he had been absolved by the bishop.

In Athens a murderer could go unpunished if no relative came forward; in the case of homicide, action could not be taken by any citizen by means of a *graphe* or public suit; a *dike* or private suit had to be brought, and could only be brought by the nearest relatives of the dead man. If a man was found guilty as the result of such a suit he was handed over to the relatives for execution. Nor could such a suit be judged by ordinary citizens, but only by the semi-religious tribunals which were presided over by the head of the national cults, the king. The most important of these ancient tribunals was the Boule of the Areopagus, which was always composed of ex-archons. At Phreattys on the sea coast were tried those who, having been temporarily exiled for unpremeditated murder, then committed a premeditated murder. As they were not yet purged of their first impurity and access to Attic territory was prohibited to them, they presented their defence from a boat, whilst their judges sat on the bank. If they were acquitted they returned to exile; if found guilty, they were executed.

Another tribunal for capital offences was constituted by the king and the kings of the tribes. It condemned by default the unknown murderer and solemnly judged any animal or inanimate object which had caused the death of a man, before purifying it or throwing it beyond the frontiers. The custom is recorded in Plato's *Laws*:

> If a beast of burden or any other animal kills anyone . . . the relatives must prosecute the killer for murder . . . if the animal is found guilty, they must kill it and throw it out beyond the frontiers of the country. If some inanimate object causes loss of human life . . . the next of kin must appoint the nearest neighbour to sit in judgment on the object, and thus affect the purification of himself and the deceased's entire line; the condemned object must be thrown over the frontier. (*Book IX*)

Although Plato speaks in terms of purification, and the pollution of a killing affected the entire city, this curious ritual must have had its origins in a wish to appease the spirit of the dead man, who was thus made to see that his kin had not failed in their duty, even though no human agent could be blamed.

That the pollution was really the result of the dead person's anger is revealed by the fact that, under Athenian law, no one could bring an action against a murderer if the victim had pardoned him before dying. The father, brothers or sons of the dead man were primarily responsible for seeking vengeance, but in their absence cousins could fulfil the duty, or ten members of the phratry appointed by the *ephetai*, the jury which took the place of the council of the Areopagus in cases of manslaughter. As in the time of private vengeance the close kinsmen might come to an arrangement with the murderer and save him from prosecution, but for the transaction to be valid it had to be accepted by all the kinsmen recognized in law.

To start an action against a murderer the kinsmen assembled round the dead man and planted a lance on the sepulchral ground, as a declaration of war. Until the day of judgment the accused was excluded from sacred places and even from the agora. The trial was held in the open air in order that those taking part might escape being infected by the impurity of the defendant, and the hearings started with animal sacrifices. If the votes were equally divided the accused had the benefit of the vote of Athene, in remembrance of the vote the goddess had given in favour of Orestes. As a rule a person accused of homicide would submit to ritual expiations and purifications to avoid temporary excommunication or exile.

Failure to fulfil the duty of a kinsman meant that the wrath of the dead man was transferred from the killer to the kinsman. He became polluted:

> Whosoever of deliberate intent and unjustly slays with his own hand any of the tribesmen shall, in the first place, be debarred from the lawful assemblies, and shall not defile either temples or markets or harbours or any other place of meeting . . . and the man who fails to prosecute him when he ought, or fails to warn him of the fact that he is thus debarred, if he be of kin to the dead man on either the male or female side, and not further removed than a cousin, shall, first, receive upon himself the defilement and wrath of the gods . . . and, secondly, he shall be liable to the action of whosoever pleases to punish him on behalf of the dead man. (*Book IX*)

Plato deals with murder and its consequences in some detail in his *Laws*, and grades the heinousness of the crime according to intent and the relationship of the killer to his victim. Matricide and parricide come top of the list:

> if 'to die a hundred deaths' were possible for any one man that a parricide or a matricide, who did the deed in rage, should undergo a hundred deaths would be a fate most just. Since every law will forbid the man to kill father or mother, the very authors of his own existence, even for the sake of saving his own life, and will ordain that he must suffer and

> endure everything rather than commit such an act,—in what other way than this can such a man be fittingly dealt with by law, and receive his due reward? Be it enacted, therefore, that for the man who in a rage slays father or mother the penalty is death. (*Ibid.*)

And, echoing the blood-feuds of fated families in Greek history and drama, he writes:

> If ever a man has slain his father, he must endure to suffer the same violent fate at his own children's hands in days to come . . . for of the pollution of common blood there is no other purification, nor does the stain of pollution admit of being washed off before the soul which committed the act pays back murder for murder. (*Ibid.*)

Plato also prescribes death for a slave who kills a free man. Rank often plays a part in the degree of pollution involved in a killing, or the amount of compensation required. For instance, Roscoe records that amongst the Baganda no punishment was inflicted on a man who speared his wife or a slave to death, since they were regarded as his property.

For the killing of a husband or wife, a brother or sister, Plato prescribes a period of exile followed by separation for life from the rest of the family. A man who has killed his wife shall, on his return from exile, 'never take part in worship with his children, nor sit at table with them; and if either the parent or the child disobeys, he shall be liable to a charge of impiety at the hands of whoso pleases'.

Plato emphasizes that there is a need for purification even when the killing was involuntary, and he knows that the reason for this is the spirit of the dead person:

> And if anyone kill a free man involuntarily, he shall undergo the same purifications as the man that has killed a slave; and there is an ancient tale, told of old, to which he must not fail to pay regard. The tale is this,—that the man slain by violence, who has lived in a free and proud spirit, is

> wroth with his slayer when newly slain, and being filled also with dread and horror on account of his own violent end, when he sees his murderer going about in the very haunts which he himself had frequented, he is horror-stricken; and being disquieted himself, he takes conscience as his ally, and with all his might disquiets his slayer—both the man himself and his doings. Wherefore it is right for the slayer to retire before his victim for a full year, in all its seasons, and to vacate all the spots he owned in all parts of his native land. (*Ibid.*)

This is a very curious blend of ancient belief and modern psychology, a blend which Shakespeare was also to achieve in English drama, particularly in *Macbeth*. Because the spirit of the dead person is all-important, Plato even excludes matricides and parricides from the death penalty if the dying victim voluntarily forgives the crime.

Pollution is automatic and has nothing to do with the malicious intent of the killer. The man who has committed an involuntary killing, says Plato, will be pardoned by the kin of the dead man if he obeys the rules of purification and avoidance:

> but if a man disobeys, and dares, in the first place, to approach the altars and to do sacrifice while still unpurified, and if he refuses, further to fulfil the times appointed in exile, then the next of kin to the dead man shall prosecute the slayer for murder. . . . And should the nearest relative fail to prosecute for the crime, it shall be as though the pollution had passed on to him. (*Ibid.*)

Surviving Greek drama takes on a new dimension once we understand how very alive these beliefs on the dead and the pollution of killing were. They were not abstractions, not poetic or literary notions. The *miasma* which surrounded a killer was as real as an infectious virus is to us. There has been a tendency to concentrate on Greek civilization as a period of enlightenment, to extract from the past values we ourselves hold dear, and to put the emphasis on philosophy and humanism, ignoring other aspects which alone help us to understand a distant civilization in its full human complexity.

We have seen that kingship involved sacred ritual, and that drama about kings provided ritual at one remove, an exemplary or secondary ritual. This secondary ritual takes on a particular importance when the primary source is no longer available—when monarchy becomes remote and centralized, for example. In the same way ritual dramas about the revenge of murdered kinsmen fulfil a secondary ritual function—ritual by example. It is significant that surviving drama deals with a past situation which no longer existed at the time when the plays were written and performed: that is, the situation where revenge was wholly the duty of the nearest kinsmen, and there was no intervening civic judiciary. Just as the 'king' of fifth-century Athens fulfilled ritual functions but exercised no political power in the way kings had once done, so the kinsmen of those who had died violently had lost the power to take direct revenge and fulfilled a mainly ritual function in setting the state machinery in motion. Thus dramas set in the past enabled a contemporary audience to understand the full meaning of the rituals in which they still participated.

Turning to Elizabethan and Jacobean drama, it is arguable that the taste for revenge drama with its attendant ghosts was at least stimulated by the abolition of ritual masses for the dead after the Reformation. Having been deprived of the Christian model for the ritual pacification of the spirits of the dead, society turned to an earlier, pagan model, at least in imagination, in the secondary ritual of the theatre, stimulated by access to earlier drama, particularly that of Seneca. This would parallel the replacement of Christ—after the suppression of the miracle cycles—by a secular drama in which the figure of the king played a semi-divine role. The reign of Elizabeth was distinguished by much political and literary propaganda surrounding the unifying, almost mythical figure of the monarch, and the Tudor myth may have had such a high degree of success because of the collapse of the old religion. Royal progresses instead of religious processions, dramas on the fate of kings instead of dramas on the life and passion of Christ.

Of the Greek drama that has survived, the *Oresteia* of Aeschylus most fully exemplifies Greek beliefs on the relationship between the living and the dead: the cycle of murder and revenge which runs through the trilogy fully bears out Plato's statement that the pollution of common blood can only be wiped out by more blood. There is no reason why the cycle of the blood-feud should not have been endless, and the ultimate intervention of Athene, who releases Orestes from the curse of his mother's blood and changes the Furies into the Eumenides, must have justified to contemporary audiences the establishment of their own judicial system. The old tribal values of kinship were upheld, but by channelling disputes through civic courts the old cycle of blood-feuds could be cut short and bloodshed could be kept to a minimum.

In the *Oresteia* the blood-feud between close kinsmen had begun long before the opening of the action itself, the point at which Aeschylus begins the trilogy. Typically, the whole trouble had begun when the brothers Atreus and Thyestes quarrelled about the succession to the throne of Argos. We have already seen that this is a situation which provides a fundamental dilemma for societies which function politically through kingship, and it is one that provides ample tragic material for drama, since such a conflict between rival claimants is liable to have an adverse effect on the peace and prosperity of the entire nation. In many of the societies studied by social anthropologists the problem was solved by putting the king's brothers or even children to death; and the murder of royal personages for the same political ends was a phenomenon not unfamiliar to Shakespeare's audiences.

The feud between the two brothers in the *Oresteia* had had terrible consequences for the people of Argos not because of civil war, but because of the pollution brought to them by the spilling of kinsmen's blood, as in the case of Oedipus at Thebes. Thyestes seduced his brother's wife, and Atreus retaliated by murdering his brother's two sons and feeding his unsuspecting brother on their flesh at a banquet. This unclean act rendered him permanently taboo in the eyes of the Argive citizens, so that he had to go into exile and could never occupy the throne.

Agamemnon is the son of Atreus and Aegisthus is the surviving son of Thyestes. When the play begins Aegisthus is not merely committing a crime when he murders Agamemnon, not simply taking over his wife and throne, he is also avenging his father. Whilst Clytemnestra is not simply being a fickle wife, she is avenging the death of her child, Iphigenia, whom Agamemnon sacrificed to the gods in order that he might have success at the war. Even without the presence of Cassandra, even without the intervention of her lover Aegisthus, there can be no reunion between Agamemnon and his queen. If a child is killed, says Plato, the husband and wife must part for good.

It is customary to talk about Fate in relation to Greek drama, but if there is any Fate in the cycle of these events it is not in the sense that we would understand it. Certain actions have inevitable consequences. Murder will follow on murder, not so much because of the all-seeing eye of heaven, not because the gods are just, but because the spirits of the dead are angry and will give the living no peace. The palace of Agamemnon is occupied by the Furies, and everybody is aware of this unpleasant fact. Clytemnestra knows it, and her hope is that the death of Agamemnon will end the vicious cycle and banish the spirits from her home. The citizens of Argos who make up the chorus also know that the palace of their king is haunted.

As a woman, Electra cannot avenge her father's death, but she does the next best thing by offering libations at her father's grave, praying for his blessing and pronouncing a curse on his murderers. Her action is motivated by fear rather than affection. Knowing that his spirit will be angry and clamouring for vengeance, she makes sure that her father will be in no doubt as to where her loyalty lies:

> *Father, let some good chance bring Orestes here! Oh listen,*
> *Answer my prayer!*
> *For myself, a pure heart and clean hands,*
> *And ways and thoughts unlike my mother's, are my request.*
> *So much for us. Next, for our enemies: let your avenger,*
> *Father, appear; let those who killed taste death for death,*

Justly! This hope I stake against my enemies' hope,
My curse to match their curse, wickedness for wickedness.
But to us, be gracious . . .

She pours her libation of wine into the earth in order, the chorus say,

To avert the evil day,
To shield the faithful head,
And hold the curse of blood at bay

and the chorus go on to make their grief apparent and to pray for the appearance of an avenger.

As nearest male kin Orestes must be the avenger. He knows, as Plato says, that if he fails to carry out this duty the anger of the dead man's spirit will turn from the guilty party on to him. This has been revealed to him by Apollo who, as the god of purification, was traditionally connected with homicide:

This was the god's command:
'Shed blood for blood, your face set like a flint. The price
They owe no wealth can weigh.' My very life, he said,
Would pay, in endless torment, for disobedience.
First he revealed what things men must perform, to soothe
Anger of spirits of earth; then, if such anger rise
What plagues break forth: the spreading scab whose rabid teeth
Eat at the flesh till human shape is gone; the white
Fungus that flowers upon the scab. But when, he said,
A father's blood lies unavenged, and time grows ripe,
The neglectful son sees yet more fearful visitations,
As, towards eyes that strain and peer in darkness, come
The attacking Furies, roused by inherited blood-guilt,
Armed with arrows of the dark, with madness, false night-terrors,
To harass, plague, torment—to scourge him forth from his city

With the brazen lash, in loathed and abject filthiness.
Banquet and wine, grace of libation, he may not share—
This was the oracle's word; his father's anger, unseen,
Bars him from every altar; no man may receive him
Or share his lodging; scorned, friendless and alone,
at length
He lies a shrivelled husk, horribly embalmed by death.

This is a horrifying description of the consequences of neglected duty. To a contemporary audience such a long-winded account of what they already knew must have acted as a moral reminder. If drama is secondary ritual, it did indeed purge by pity and terror. The audience knew that Orestes was speaking the truth, that he had no choice but to avenge his father's death, and yet matricide would also have terrible consequences. Clytemnestra uses this knowledge to avert her own death when she tell Orestes to 'Beware the hounding Furies of a mother's curse', but he retorts that, were he to do so, he would only have his father's curse to contend with instead.

After the death of Clytemnestra the trilogy turns into an argument about kinship which is finally resolved by Athene. The Furies, spurred into action by the ghost of Clytemnestra, engage in an argument with Apollo in which they claim that the murder of a husband by a wife is not so bad as a son killing his mother, since the former involves no blood relationship. Apollo argues that the marriage bond is more sacred than an oath, but Athene settles the matter on patriarchal grounds when she gives her casting vote, claiming 'male supremacy in all things'. Apollo, who appears at the court of the Areopagus on behalf of Orestes, since the latter has gone to his temple for purification, also makes a patriarchal claim:

The mother is not the true parent of the child
Which is called hers. She is a nurse who tends the growth
Of young seed planted by its true parent, the male.

Since the ultimate aim of Athenian drama is to glorify Athens and her institutions, the triumphant Orestes swears that, should any future Argive king turn against Attica, he himself will rise from the grave in vengeance. Thus the play not only gave the audience an *aeton* or origin for the Athenian court which dealt with homicide, but gave it an added assurance: the spirit of the dead Orestes would seek vengeance against Argos if it ever dared to attack Athens. Athene reconciles the old kinship claims, personified by the Furies, who claim that the ancient tribal laws are being ignored and that plague and disaster will follow with the new civic authority; Athene promises that the old gods will still be worshipped and begs them not to bring civic strife by setting man against man: 'Let war be with the stranger, at the stranger's gate.' The Furies are ultimately mollified, accept an honoured place in the new scheme of things, and turn into the Eumenides, who pour blessings on the people of Athens. 'God and Fate are reconciled.'

In England the rival claims of kinsmen, with their feuds, and the claims of the city, are best exemplified by *Romeo and Juliet*. Had the two families not engaged in a blood-feud, their beloved children would not have died so tragically: this is the message at the end of the play. Machiavelli's *Florentine History* appeared in English translation in 1595, the same year as Shakespeare wrote *Romeo and Juliet*. Machiavelli discourses on the dangers of factions within the city when powerful families quarrel, and gives the families Albizi and Ricci as examples:

> These two houses hating one the other, studied how they might oppresse the other . . . there happened by chaunce a quarrell in the olde Market . . . During the brunt of this brute, newes were brought to the Ricci, that the Albizi assailed them. And in like manner it was told to the Albizi, that the Ricci sought for them. Upon these rumours, all the citie arose, and the Magistrates could with difficultie hold backe the one and the other of these families, from dooing of that violence, which without any fault or intent of theirs, was occasioned.

In his introduction Machiavelli claims that the greatness of Florence is proved by the fact that it could survive 'so many murthers, so many banishments, and so many subversions of Families'.

Only a small fraction of Aeschylus's work has survived, but his deep concern with the old religious laws is also evident in his other surviving plays. In *Seven Against Thebes*, for instance, a similar curse passes down the house of Oedipus from generation to generation, until the polluted family is wiped out. By the time we get to Sophocles, however, the emphasis is no longer on religious ritual but on human emotion. His Electra's grief is one of human loss and deprivation, not primarily a ritual duty to the dead, and her hatred is real too, not firstly inspired by fear of an angry spirit. The libation scene at the grave of Agamemnon has disappeared, and the action takes place outside the palace, when Electra sees her sister come out with a libation from her mother, who has had a bad dream. Electra has been forbidden to leave the house, and she tells her sister to throw the libation away and offer locks of hair from both of them instead:

> *Kneel to him*
> *And pray that he himself will come from the dead*
> *To befriend us and help us against our enemies;*
> *And that Orestes may be alive and coming in strength*
> *To crush his father's enemies under his foot;*

But the ritual no longer has such central importance, otherwise it would have been dramatized; and Electra would have performed it herself, instead of leaving it to her timid sister. No mere prohibition from her mother would have stopped her. When it comes to it, she does not lack courage and initiative. When she believes Orestes to be dead she suggests that she and her sister should kill Aegisthus, but it is significant that she makes the suggestion not just as a pious duty to their dead father, but because the alternative would appear to be lifelong spinsterhood, with both deprived of their just inheritance. Their father's death may be the justification, but their own situation is the true reason. In this play there is no curse on the house, the palace is not haunted by Furies, but Electra points out that such a killing would be honoured by the people. In other words, they would get away with it. And when Clytemnestra prays to Apollo she prays to be saved from the ill will of the living, from those who may be plotting against her, and not from the anger of the spirits, even though she has had a symbolic dream which prompted her to send a libation at her daughter's hands. Again one feels, why did she not go herself, if Agamemnon's spirit was really the greatest danger? The ritual is demeaned by the main protagonists, and thus also in the eyes of the audience, by being assigned to a rather peripheral and slightly contemptible character, the timid and conformist sister. The real drama in this play takes place between the living.

Ghosts were a very popular feature in Elizabethan and Jacobean drama, and literary historians often claim that English dramatists 'stole' this device from Seneca. Although Seneca was read and imitated, we must also ask why they copied this device. It is not enough to say that ghosts are theatrically effective, since theatrical effect depends on audience response. If one has no inclination to believe in ghosts a theatrical spook is more like to raise a laugh than a shudder, particularly without the aid of modern lighting techniques. One must assume that contemporary audiences had a strong tendency to believe in ghosts, and this is confirmed by the literature of the period, even though the belief was questioned in some quarters.

The Protestant Reformation had abolished masses for the souls of the dead, which had been a lucrative source of revenue for the Catholic Church. Official Protestant theology proclaimed that Purgatory did not exist, and that souls did not come back from the dead to require ritual expiation from the living. In that case—what were ghosts? People do not abandon their beliefs and superstitions overnight to conform with ecclesiastical policy, and would not at once stop seeing spectres in dark corners, or hear things go bump in the night. Such manifestation had to be explained. Throughout the latter half of the sixteenth century there was a lively debate going on as to whether ghosts existed at all and if so, what kind of manifestations they were. Even Reginald Scot, who was remarkably sceptical for his time, was not prepared to dismiss the idea of spirits altogether. On the whole it was felt that, since the souls of the dead went straight to Heaven or Hell, apparitions must either be figments of the imagination or sent by the Devil. There was some doubt as to whether they could also be sent from God and, although the possibility was not entirely ruled out, Protestant writers were inclined to doubt it. They tended to think that divine apparitions straight from the Almighty belonged only to Biblical times, and that the age of miracles was past.

If an apparition was a figment of the imagination this could be because the person thus haunted was particularly timorous and fearful, a woman for example, but it was most likely to happen because the person who saw the ghost was (like Hamlet) suffering from melancholy. Lavater, in *Of Ghostes and Spirites Walking by Nyght*, James I in his *Daemonologie*, and Reginald Scot in *The Discoverie of Witchcraft*, are all agreed on this point. 'Melancholike persons, and madde men, imagine many things which in verie deede are not,' writes Lavater, and goes on to say that 'Madde men which have utterly loste the use of reason, or are vexed by Gods permission with a Divell' are thus afflicted. 'Fearful men imagine that they see and heare straunge things,' he writes, adding that men with murder on their conscience are liable to see apparitions. The ambivalence of Banquo's ghost, which is seen by Macbeth and none of the other guests at the banquet, must have been particularly striking for a contemporary audience.

But it is as a source book for *Hamlet*, where the ghost serves to trigger off the entire action, that Lavater's work is most interesting. He denounces the concept of Purgatory as a Popish device for extorting money from surviving kin, and gives examples of manifestations fraudulently manufactured by Popish priests. But this is not to say that such apparitions do not exist, because 'it is no difficult matter for the devil to appeare in divers shapes, not only of those which are alive, but also of deade menne'. When Hamlet sees the ghost he immediately questions him:

> *Be thou a spirit of health or goblin damn'd,*
> *Bring with thee airs from heaven or blasts from hell,*
> *Be thy intents wicked or charitable,*

and when he later decides to test the ghost's veracity by putting on a play he says:

> *The spirit that I have seen*
> *May be the devil: and the devil hath power*
> *To assume a pleasing shape; yea, and perhaps*
> *Out of my weakness and my melancholy—*
> *As he is very potent with such spirits—*
> *Abuses me to damn me.*

When, after seeing the ghost, Hamlet tells Horatio that he'll go and pray, he is also following Lavater's advice:

> It behoveth them which are vexed with spirits, to pray especially, and to give themselves to fasting, sobrietie, watching, and upright and godly living.

And we are reminded of the soldier who tries to attack the ghost on the ramparts with his sword when we read Lavater: 'We must not use a materiall sword against spirits and vayne shewes . . . but we must use the sword of the Spirit'.

But although Lavater warns his readers to be very suspicious of apparitions, he is not prepared to rule out entirely the possibility that spirits may have a good purpose, as proves to be the case in *Hamlet*: 'God doth suffer Spirites to appeare unto his electe unto a goode ende, but unto the reprobate they appeare as a punishment.' In spite of the new Protestantism he has not discarded the divine framework within which tragedians were able to work:

> In that there happeneth certayne straunge things before the death of men, and also before notable alterations, and the destructions of countries, as marvellous crackes, & terrible roaring, surely it turneth to good unto the just, & to further

damnation to the wicked. For by these means God sheweth that nothing commeth to passe by chaunce, or by adventure, but that the life and dethe, the prosperous or unfortunate estate of al men, is in the power and hand of God.

Macbeth, *Hamlet* and *King Lear* all function within this superstitious framework of belief, and all show symptoms of the ambivalence and uncertainty we find in Lavater, which Shakespeare also expresses but puts to good dramatic use. In *Macbeth* you can scoff with Lady Macbeth or tremble with her husband when the ghost of Banquo appears; in *Hamlet* it is also possible to side with various characters in the interpretation of the apparition. In *King Lear* one may laugh with Edmund at the superstitious belief in portents displayed by Gloucester, but when all is said and done Edmund is the villain, and the good Edgar exploits his father's superstitious nature quite shamelessly, after he has been blinded, to restore Gloucester's faith in a higher justice. The kind of imagery Edgar uses, both as 'poor Tom', and at the imaginary cliff when describing 'poor Tom' as a fiend, is listed as the direst superstition (but in great detail) by Scot in *The Discoverie of Witchcraft*:

> The first and principall king (which is the power of the east) is called *Baell*; who when he is conjured up, appeareth with three heads; the first, like a tode; the second like a man; the third like a cat. He speaketh with a hoarse voice, he maketh a man go invisible, and he hath under his obedience and rule sixty and six legions of divels.

> Balam is a great and terrible king, he commeth forth with three heads, the first of a bull, the second of a man, and the third of a ram, he hath a serpents taile, and flaming eyes, riding upon a furious beare, and carrying a hawke on his fist, he speaketh with a hoarse voice . . .

Scot declares that anyone who believes that such apparitions and spirits exist 'may soone be brought to believe that the moone is made of green cheese'; nevertheless the descriptions go on for many pages, suggesting that they were far from having lost all credibility in the minds of a great sector of the population. He also stresses that 'Many through melancholy doe imagine, that they see or hear visions, spirits, ghosts, strange noises &c. Many again through fear proceeding from a cowardly nature and complexion . . . are timerous and afraid of spirits.' He is somewhat disinclined to believe that ghosts can be sent by the Devil, though he finally declines to reach a firm conclusion by asserting that the whole topic is fraught with difficulty, and that no one has yet written convincingly on the subject. Like Lavater, but with rather more scepticism, he mentions the belief that there are spirits in the mines (Hamlet's 'old mole'). However, it is important to realize that neither Lavater nor even Reginald Scot are sceptics by modern standards, only by the standards of their own day.

So the ambivalence which we find in *King Lear* with regard to superstitious portents was characteristic of the period. It is also important to remember that by the time Shakespeare wrote *King Lear* Reginald Scot was in disgrace owing to the accession of James I, who had the book publicly burned. Who knows—perhaps the artificial ravings of 'poor Tom' contain a hidden joke against an eminent personage whose notoriously superstitious nature had been so successfully pandered to in *Macbeth*?

However, it is certain that the very real doubts and fears that surrounded such topics in the sixteenth and early seventeenth century gave an excellent opportunity to the dramatist. The question of supernatural manifestations was highly controversial, and the ambiguity which surrounded the whole subject made for a great dramatic tension both at a philosophical and an entertainment level. One could say that the audiences were tasting of forbidden fruits, since the new religion discouraged a belief in ghosts, and that dramatists were pandering to a natural appetite which had been frustrated in other directions.

The doubts which surrounded supernatural manifestations are crucial to an understanding of *Hamlet*, where the ghost is of central importance and where the main protagonist is required to take drastic action on information received from the ghost.

Horatio represents the contemporary position on the matter, uneasy and vacillating. He starts off as a sceptic who believes the apparition to be a fantasy, but when he sees the ghost himself his scepticism is shaken. 'This bodes some strange eruption to our state,' he says, in conformity with Lavater, but later he becomes less certain. When Hamlet intends to follow the ghost he warns him that the apparition may lead him to his death or madness; when Marcello tells him of spirits and witchcraft he says: 'So I have heard and do in part believe it', which just about sums up the contemporary attitude. Although Hamlet tells Horatio that his philosophy is inadequate he is obviously in some doubt himself, and some of these doubts are expressed in the 'To be, or not to be' soliloquy: although he refers to

The undiscover'd country from whose bourn
No traveller returns

which is the Protestant view, his father's ghost has made it quite clear that he has come back from Purgatory, doomed to walk the earth until his murder has been revenged: thus the 'dread of something after death' takes on a new dimension.

Apparitions can also be used for prophecy, for reasons which have already been discussed; it is not only *Macbeth* which endorses the view of James I that true prophecy belongs to God and that the powers of the Devil and his agents in this respect are limited. Like Macbeth, the chief protagonist in George Chapman's *Bussy d'Ambois* gets ambiguous replies from the spirits he has raised from Hell to tell him what the future holds for him. With God's permission such misleading prophecies lead the wicked to their own destruction. The parade of kings in *Macbeth* does not conform to this doctrine, but we have already seen that there were political motives for this scene.

James I also took the view that the Devil was behind most apparitions. The Devil, he says, tends to attack those of weak faith, which is why, he conveniently explains, there were a lot of ghosts during Popish times but now that Christians have reformed their Church they are hardly seen at all. Which is a rather different viewpoint from that of Reginald Scot. 'Where are the soules that swarmed in times past?' asks Scot. 'Are they all gone into Italy, because masses are growne deere here in England?' The Devil, writes James, is liable to attack us with ghosts when we are particularly weak, that is, alone and fearful in some solitary place, but he does not rule out the idea of divine purpose altogether: 'On the other parte, when he troubles certaine houses that are dwelt in, it is a sure token either of grosse ignorance, or of some grosse and slanderous sinnes amongst the inhabitants thereof: which God by that extra-ordinarie rod punishes.'

Scot, in spite of his essential scepticism, was ultimately uncertain about supernatural beings; James, in spite of his strong superstition, was ultimately uncertain about the interpretation that should be put upon supernatural manifestations. This uncertainty must have given a quite peculiar tension to the appearances of spectres and apparitions on the contemporary stage, and the probability that they were demonic must have been a large part of their attraction, and given the audience a pleasurable thrill of horror. But it needed a master like Shakespeare to explore the more sophisticated ambivalence, not between God and the Devil, but between the beginnings of a psychological approach and the old medieval framework of belief. He gives us such a melancholy Hamlet, such a guilt-ridden Macbeth, that twentieth-century readers are able to accept these plays within modern terms of reference and are, if anything, liable to ignore or underestimate the attitudes of a society that had adapted rather than rejected the beliefs of the Middle Ages, and had a very lively interest in necromancy and the supernatural. The fact that such beliefs were no longer contained within Church orthodoxy, since the reformed Church had to a large extent rejected the beliefs and abandoned the concomitant ritual, allowed the secular interest to flourish as never before. Learned men of letters might discuss their doubts, but in doing so also betrayed their interest. The dividing line between science and magic was indistinct, and the lay population took over the ritual no longer practised by the priesthood. The eventual backlash would come in the form of witch-hunts. By our standards ancient beliefs had not been rejected at all; there was simply an argument about their exact nature, about definitions and limitations, and argument fosters interest. No wonder this interest is reflected in the drama of the period.

Incidentally, it is interesting that the belief that the forgiveness of the victim absolves the murderer should have survived, at least in literary form, as late as Shakespeare's time. As Hamlet and Laertes lie dying the latter says:

> *Exchange forgiveness with me, noble Hamlet:*
> *Mine and my father's death come not upon thee,*
> *Nor thine on me!*

Laertes expires immediately after these words, whereupon Hamlet exclaims:

> *Heaven make thee free of it!*

presumably because he is too late to do so. Forgiveness pronounced by the dying also appears in other plays of the period, in *Bussy d'Ambois*, for instance. Such forgiveness ends the cycle of the blood-feud, since there is then no angry spirit to be appeased. It will be remembered that under Greek law a murderer could not be prosecuted if his victim had forgiven him before dying. Thus, in Euripides' play *Hippolytus*, Hippolytus absolves his father of his death before dying, at the request of Theseus, who asks, 'And will you leave me guilty and defiled?' whereupon his son absolves him.

The status of the ghost in *Hamlet* is not the only ambiguity in the play: throughout the play we have an exploration of semblance and reality. Nothing is quite what it seems, people pretend to be what they are not, and it is more difficult than one might suppose to tell a hawk from a handsaw. Gertrude is a 'most seeming-virtuous queen', Claudius pretends to be what he is not and Hamlet, in order to carry out his plan and survive in the process, pretends to be mad, as Edgar pretends to be mad in order to survive in *King Lear*. Poor Ophelia comes to grief because she is not cunning enough to see through pretences, and because she does not pick up the clue given to her in the love poem which, in any other context, would be trite enough, but in this context has to be read very carefully indeed:

Doubt thou the stars are fire;
Doubt that the sun doth move;
Doubt truth to be a liar;
But never doubt I love.

Modern critics, with their penchant for psycho-analysis, have tended to see Hamlet as the bearer of a massive Freudian Oedipus complex; ie, Hamlet sees the ghost because he really wanted to kill his father, and he now wants to kill Claudius in order to marry his mother. Once this ludicrous interpretation has been accepted it is easy to assume that Hamlet, far from pretending to be mad, really is crazy. Such doubts can be clarified by a consideration of Kyd's *The Spanish Tragedy*, usually considered the first Elizabethan revenge tragedy, the success of which helped to inspire the spate of later works on the same theme. In *The Spanish Tragedy* Kyd gets round the problem of the abolition of Purgatory by making his ghost ascend from the pagan underworld, described at length in a passage adapted from the *Aeneid*, but which sounds odd in the mouth of the ghost of a Spanish nobleman who was presumably a Catholic during his lifetime, an embarrassing fact which is tactfully ignored. In this play Hieronimo, like Hamlet, takes a long time to revenge his son's death; like Hamlet he knows himself to be in a court where he must be constantly on his guard and where he can trust no one; like Hamlet he blames himself for his own procrastination, contemplates suicide and rejects it because his son must be avenged; like Hamlet he is considered mad by the court, who believe him to be distracted and crazed by grief—as a result they do not consider him a serious threat. But when Hieronimo is alone on stage his soliloquys, like those of Hamlet, are remarkably sane. Finally, like Hamlet, he gets his revenge by means of a play within the play, one which exactly parallels the crime which is being revenged, but in this play the villains—who think they are merely acting—are really stabbed to death before the court audience. Hieronimo is an honest machiavell, like Hamlet, and knows that cunning must be matched with cunning if justice is to prevail in the end:

> *Wise men will take their opportunity*
> *Closely and safely, fitting things to time.*

Hieronimo and Hamlet both know that it is necessary to dissemble (as Hieronimo tells his wife to do) until the right opportunity comes along.

And this brings us to a consideration of the political implications of revenge tragedy. The Greeks also tended to put divine sanctions on crimes which could not easily be detected or punished by human agency, but during Shakespeare's lifetime there were very particular reasons for introducing the ghosts of murdered noblemen and princes, in particular, and for showing the audience (in the words of Hieronimo's wife, which are echoed in so many of Shakespeare's plays) that

> *The heav'ns are just; murder cannot be hid:*
> *Time is the author both of truth and right,*
> *And time will bring this treachery to light.*

Murder as a political weapon was nothing new, but Shakespeare's contemporaries had been shocked by the writings of Machiavelli, who appeared to justify political expediency. Political expediency was nothing new either, but to condone and even recommend it was quite another matter. Ghosts therefore reinforced the old framework of divine retribution, even though plays like *Hamlet* and *The Spanish Tragedy* recognize that good men must be able to outwit the bad for justice to triumph in the end. *The Revenger's Tragedy* by Tourneur also shows us a court where everybody is corrupt; the revenger, Vindice, has to revenge the poisoning of his betrothed by the old Duke, who has just married his mother. Vindice knows that the court is an immoral place, full of 'politicians' anxious for power and preferment, and that he must be cunning to achieve his purpose, so he constantly adopts disguises and pretends to be a villain himself. Significantly, the play is set at an Italian court, and throughout the play we are constantly being told that all men are corrupt and all women are unchaste. In this play the mother, like Hamlet's mother, is unchaste, the daughter, like Ophelia, is good, but the virtuous girl is told that she is being very foolish in a world where 'All thrives but chastity'. As for political loyalties:

> *Faiths are bought and sold;*
> *Oaths in these days are but the skin of gold.*

When Vindice disguises himself as a villain he is introduced in the following manner:

> *My lord, after long search, wary inquiries,*
> *And politic siftings, I made choice of yon fellow,*
> *Whom I guess rare for many deep employments;*
> *This our age swims within him, and if time*
> *Had so much hair, I should take him for time.*
> *He is so near kin to this present minute.*

In such a world the moral principle that 'murder will out', which is expressed in every tragedy of the period, just as it is expressed in all Greek tragedies, cannot be fulfilled sometimes without the assistance of ghosts. The murder of Hamlet's father was so cunningly carried out that there was no possibility of detection without a supernatural apparition to tell all. The villain in Tourneur's *Atheist's Tragedy* goes about his business with equal cunning, so that

> *nothing from*
> *Th' induction to th' accomplishment seem'd forc'd*
> *Or done o' purpose, but by accident.*

With such a villain this play also requires a ghost to reveal the truth; Charlemont is far from home when his old father 'accidentally' slips down a gravel pit, and so it is his ghost who tells him that he was in actual fact murdered, just as Hamlet needs his father's ghost to tell him that he did not die of a snakebite. Like Hamlet, Charlemont tends to doubt the evidence of his senses, and it requires a second appearance, with a soldier vainly trying to shoot the apparition with his musket, as the soldier in *Hamlet* tries to use a sword, to convince him that the ghost is genuine and that the murder must be revenged. Faced with the Machiavellian philosophy of politics (or what they imagined that philosophy to be, since *The Prince* was not translated until 1640) the supernatural, in spite of its theological ambiguities, must at the same time have reinforced the notion that there is justice in the world and that crime inevitably meets with retribution.

Although *Macbeth* works well as a psychological drama of fear, that fear depends upon a belief in the supernatural. Soon after the murder Macbeth is worried by his inability to utter the word 'Amen', and the appearance of Banquo's ghost provokes him to remember that:

> *It will have blood, they say; blood will have blood:*
> *Stones have been known to move and trees to speak;*
> *Augurs and understood relations have*
> *By maggot pies and choughs and rooks brought forth*
> *The secret'st man of blood.*

Lady Macbeth is the character who seems least prone to worry about superstition and the supernatural, she scoffs at her husband's fears and believes that 'A little water clears us of this deed'. But Macbeth *has* murdered sleep, and by the sleepwalking scene Lady Macbeth knows that all the perfumes of Arabia will not wash the blood off her hands—like Clytemnestra she is haunted by dreams, and it must be remembered that apparitions in dreams were believed to be ghosts also. So, although Lady Macbeth does not see Banquo at the feast, the ghosts reach her too, and deny her rest. The doctor who sees her thus haunted knows that 'This disease is beyond my practice. . . . More needs she the divine than the physician.' But there is no absolution for murder except in death; in her haunted sleep she knows what she denies in her waking hours, that her hands will ne'er be clean.

4 Women

Spencer and Gillen reported that there were two types of ceremony performed by the aborigine tribes they studied—ceremonies which might be witnessed, and perhaps taken part in by women and even children; and those which only initiated men could see and participate in. The great majority of the latter were connected with the totems, and referred to episodes in the lives of the totemic ancestors. Even though some of these ancestors may have been female, their parts were performed by men.

The tribes studied by Spencer and Gillen give us a picture of patriarchy in its most primitive but also its most obvious form, and the two men had no doubt about what they were witnessing—a collusion between men which enabled them to maintain control. Ceremonial, mystique and mystery, these were in the hands of men, who therefore exercised power. In describing mortuary ceremonies the authors mention briefly and in passing that the Binbinga tribe ate their dead, but that women did not take part in this. Again, women are excluded from the continuity of the tribe, its power, since eating the flesh of the dead involves a belief that in doing so one takes into onself the power and special qualities of the dead person.

Amongst the tribes described by Spencer and Gillen women were excluded from most of the important rituals related to the life of the tribe, its corporate and sacred history which, being performed in groups and thus influencing the present and future, presented a living continuum. It is important to realize that sacred ritual recreates, as, for instance, the Last Supper is recreated during Christian communion, so that the wafer becomes the body of Christ, and the wine drunk by the communicants, his blood. The function of women during these tribal performances was to be fearful and awed witnesses (though not actually present) of the sacred power exercised by men, just as, in the history of the Christian Church, they made an obedient and pious audience but were totally excluded from any sacerdotal or even subsidiary ritual function.

The power of ritual on the audience is to some extent reinforced by secrecy. The high altar is partially hidden from worshippers by an elaborate rood screen. And what really goes on in the vestry, from which the priest and his minions emerge? As has already been said, amongst the aborigine tribes the storehouses of the sacred churinga—holy stones or pieces of wood connected with the spiritual continuity of the tribe—were never visited by the women who, unless they were very old, were not even supposed to know of their existence. The women were required to make considerable detours to avoid coming within the vicinity, which suggests some knowledge of their whereabouts. Initiated boys were given their churinga and told that they must on no account show it to the women or children. The women believed the sound made by swinging the churinga to be a spirit, but the initiated boys, having joined the men, now knew that this 'spirit' was only a mechanical invention to keep women and children in order.

There is nothing unique about this exclusion of women from important ritual function. It is common in other societies which have been studied by anthropologists and it could perhaps be regarded as the foundation stone of patriarchy in the social evolutionary process. Christian, Judaic and Islamic ritual is performed by men, and the function of women—in so far as they have any at all—is to be witnesses, the audience. They may receive blessing or forgiveness, but not give it. It is a male function to enforce taboos and remove pollution through ritual, and in this way woman becomes subject to a male moral order.

Women are excluded from the mysteries, which can help to enforce their pious adherence. Like the aborigine men with their churinga, New Guinea males produce magical and eerie noises on musical instruments which the women are not allowed to see, and they also build elaborate chapels behind screens so that the women cannot see them until the work is finished. Evans-Pritchard, writing about the Nuer, said that women did not make sacrifices, that they could assist in the act of consecration with ashes, and they might pray, but they did not make invocations or slay victims.

When we consider the history of the Christian Church, it is significant that it was the various Puritan sects who first allowed women to have some kind of voice within the Church. St Paul had commanded women to be silent, and it was not until the sacerdotal function of the priesthood had been abolished by the Puritans that it became possible for a woman to raise her voice during a religious assembly. Significantly, this coincided with a much more egalitarian attitude to marriage. It was also during this century, particularly after the Restoration, that women began to act on the commercial stage. Sacerdotal function implies hierarchy, and in patriarchal societies that function is exclusively male. In so far as the English commercial theatre was an offshoot and development from religious drama, it was natural that it should continue to be performed exclusively by male actors until such time as there was a radical change in society itself. This came with the rise of capitalism, the breaking of the old social order, and the new religion.

Athenian women were not totally excluded from religious ritual; indeed, one particular ritual, the Festival of Thesmophoria, was celebrated exclusively by women, although the fact that Aristophanes was allowed to write a funny play about it (*The Poet and the Women*) would seem to indicate that men did not take it very seriously and did, indeed, regard these secret female rites each October as a bit of a joke. Women were, however, excluded from participation in the most important social ritual of the time: they were not citizens and took no part in the political and judicial assemblies. It was strictly a one-sex democracy. Neither did they participate (except as audience) in the dramatic festivals which were regarded as equal in importance to, and, in a sense, an adjunct to, the political dramas of the assembly.

Just as the female ancestors of the ant totem were performed by men, so Pallas Athene, Medea and Clytemnestra, all the great figures of Greek ancestral history, were performed by men, and had their lines scripted by men. And it must be remembered that Greek drama, like that of the aborigine tribes, was strongly ritualistic in character—in its form very obviously, but also in social intention. Performances were accompanied by religious sacrifices, the stories were always basically the same and celebrated the origin of some ancient religious rite, the basic structure of the drama was always the same and the preparation and execution of the dramatic festivals involved the whole community.

Japan, a country of very strong patriarchal tradition, still has a traditional drama which goes back in time to a feudal society, which is religious and ritualistic in character and where the female characters are played by men in masks. Watching Noh theatre, one feels that in many ways Greek drama must have been rather like this: the high religious tone, the set number of actors and prescribed format, the stylized performance, and the combination of music and words and dance. Like the Athenian dramatic festivals, Noh theatre is a lengthy business, and in both the tension of high religious seriousness is relieved by low comedy. Both types of drama are also hierarchical: they give us a world picture where acceptance of the social hierarchy is an essential ingredient of human piety. Thus comedies, the Japanese *kyogen* or the Greek satire, break the tension of high drama and provide some light relief: it is significant that in doing so they often have themes of status-reversal, where servants take over from masters for an hour or a day, the young are irreverent to the old, and women show defiance towards their husbands or fathers. But like rituals of status-reversal in everyday life, such scenes do in fact emphasize rather than undermine the normal hierarchy.

The submission of women is a fundamental ingredient in the hierarchy, and nothing is more symptomatic of patriarchal attitudes than a theatre where the female parts are played by men or boys. The plays themselves do of course emphasize the position of women, the virtues of obedience and chastity, for instance, but the fact that female roles are played by men adds to the male definition of femininity. When men play women they always exaggerate, sometimes to the point of absurdity, the so-called feminine traits. We have only to think of modern drag artists. No doubt the old comedians in fifth-century Athens or at the Globe nearly four hundred years ago made their audiences guffaw in a similar fashion. But the exaggeration of femininity is not confined to comedy. I have seen a Japanese actor playing a tragic Noh role, masked and dressed as a woman, and the performance was marked by an exaggerated expression of submission, gentleness and suffering (the actor was famous for his female roles). Thus the male actor, his lines written by a man, gives both men and women an idealized vision of how, according to men, the good women should behave, and an equally distorted picture of the bad woman—unchaste, disobedient and rebellious. The shrew, the nagging wife, the adulteress—no doubt they betrayed themselves just as surely, when played by men, as the good woman showed her virtue by bowed head and folded hands.

The male impersonation of women has not been sufficiently taken into account in the assessment of the great female roles, or in considering the political and social function of drama as a whole. Even in the case of Shakespeare, where an enormous body of textual and general criticism exists, this aspect of his work has been conspicuously ignored. Not, of course, in the comedies, because in these Shakespeare himself draws attention to the fact by his jokes about boys playing girls playing boys. Critics have had a field-day exploring the sexual and, at times, supposed homosexual innuendoes of the comedies, but the fact that Cordelia and Desdemona were also played by boys has been ignored, and no critical conclusions, psycho-sexual or otherwise, have been drawn.

It is also surprising how often Shakespearian commentators tell us that Shakespeare put Rosalind or Viola in trousers because it got over the difficulty of having a girl played by a boy.

But this is surely absurd, or why did he not find some excuse for putting Ophelia or Desdemona in trousers? A much more likely explanation, if we need one at all, is to assume that Shakespeare knew he was dealing with a theatrical convention and chose to poke fun at it, and at the same time exploited the joke to its full extent. Certainly he must have been aware of the practical difficulties involved in using boy actors: we know he was fully aware of the nuisance of boys' voices breaking from Hamlet's address to the players. But that the secular theatre was striving towards a new naturalism and was, for the time being, merely lumbered with old prejudices and the old liturgical tradition, is borne out by the fact that the boys were not castrated to maintain the purity of their soprano voices.

If we regard the performance of women's roles by men as highly significant, and not merely some sort of social 'accident' or superficial convention, then the moment at which women begin to step on to the boards to play themselves is also highly significant, both from a social point of view and for the study of drama within a society. Very soon after Shakespeare's day women began to perform female roles, but even to this day they are almost entirely excluded from scripting those roles. In the seventeenth century the lack of female dramatists could be explained by female illiteracy (though actresses must have been able to read, one presumes, if only to learn their lines!) but no such explanation is available today. I do not believe that it is enough to assert that women have a talent for writing novels but somehow have no gift for writing drama. We know that women's success in novel-writing was largely the result of the anonymity of the novel writer, who can use a male pseudonym and send his or her script in by post. But theatre and, in this century, film, require a much higher degree of group consensus than the publication of a novel. Directors, managers and financial backers are involved, and in the latter half of the twentieth century these are still almost invariably men. As a result women are exploited as sexual objects in theatre and cinema, and a girl can get a long way in the theatrical profession if she has the right kind of looks and is prepared to display her physical attributes to the best advantage. It was this, in the changed atmosphere of the Restoration, that made them a success on the boards in the first place.

It is now generally agreed that women can act—at least, that they can and should act female roles (though the idea of a woman playing Hamlet is still regarded as an oddity). But there is still a strong prejudice against women in a more controlling position, and particularly against female dramatists, because any woman writer who is worth anything would present an image of women, and perhaps even more devastatingly, an image of men, which does not fit in with the male consensus on what men and women are really like. When a male dramatist, like Ibsen, for instance, presents a woman in an unstereotyped and therefore shocking light, the reaction is hostile enough. When a woman, say Caryl Churchill, portrays women with the same capacity for violence as men the critics can dismiss her as someone who does not know her craft. Most would-be women dramatists are dismissed in that fashion in embryo, and never get as far as a theatrical production at all. In considering this question of group consensus, we also have to remember that writing and reading a novel is a much more private activity: this makes the expression of unconventional views more acceptable, and even perhaps more comprehensible. Shocking events appear more shocking when enacted before our eyes, and unconventional behaviour more unconventional. Actors can be made uncomfortable, the audience as a group can be made so by statements which, as private individuals, in the privacy of their own homes, they might be much more prepared to accept as valid and truthful.

The overthrow of patriarchy is a long business, and it cannot be regarded as anywhere near completion whilst drama, which has a central function in shaping and perpetuating a social ideology, is still the work of men, even if women are allowed to speak the words which have been scripted for them. Greek women never even got as far as speaking their own lines because their civilization was disrupted before the progress of enlightenment could take its course, as civilizations are apt to be. But there is certainly a marked change between the strongly moral tone of Aeschylus, with his unquestioning belief in patriarchal authority, and Euripides, who was very sympathetic to the plight of women in Greek society. Euripides was of course considered decadent (possibly, like Socrates, he was even tried for heresy) and Aristophanes certainly made it very clear that in his view only Aeschylus, and not Euripides, had the moral message which could save the city.

However far apart in time and place, Euripides and Ibsen could shock contemporary opinion, and run contrary to the patriarchal attitudes of their fellow men by not only showing sympathy for the oppression of women, but an imaginative empathy which went beyond feminist propaganda and allowed them to break the mould of the female stereotype and create something more than a pathetic victim appealing for sympathy or an attractive minx with a pert tongue in her head. In patriarchal drama the opposite of the good woman, the potential victim, is the monster, essentially unfeminine, a deformity of nature. The imaginative breakthrough which both Euripides and Ibsen made was to see that a woman could behave in a monstrous fashion and still be a woman. It is precisely for this reason that Ibsen's audiences found *Hedda Gabler* such a shocking creation, and that no doubt Athenians were shocked by the *Medea* of Euripides. It is the reason why these two plays can still arouse hostility in men today, or at least, lack of understanding.

In versions of the Medea legend prior to Euripides Medea's children had been murdered by the people of Corinth. It was the empathy that Euripides felt for women, for their helplessness in a world where men alone made the rules and broke them, that allowed him enough insight into the reality of the situation to make a daring innovation and have Medea murder her own children. It is a shocking act, one that goes against all the patriarchal tenets of woman and motherhood, but it is the one sure way in which Medea can hit back at her defecting husband, and it is by no means uncommon in our own society for women to take out their angers and frustrations on their children. Euripides had made an imaginative breakthrough by asking himself not, how would a woman behave in such a situation? but: how would *I*, how would anyone behave in such a situation? Just as

Ibsen had asked himself, when embarking on *Hedda Gabler*, how would *I* feel if I had been born into this society as a woman? As a result both dramatists attributed the capacity for violence and frustration which society recognizes in men, and which both dramatists recognized in themselves, to their female characters, and created characters which were, and to some extent still are, unacceptable in so far as they ascribe 'unfeminine' characteristics to women.

The similarity between *Hedda Gabler* and the *Medea* of Euripides is in fact very striking. The social situation of women was certainly comparable during the periods when the two dramatists were working, but the parallels are such that I feel tempted to believe that Ibsen may have been consciously or unconsciously drawing on the earlier play. Like Medea, Hedda destroys two children, the foetus in her own womb when she kills herself, and Løvborg's manuscript, which is also regarded as a child—the only question being whether Mrs Elvsted or Hedda can be regarded as the true mother. The destruction of the manuscript is the most shocking act which Hedda commits, somehow far more devastating than her final suicide. It represents the destruction of male achievement, just as the murder of the children in *Medea* represents the destruction of man's heirs—the Greek view of reproduction was that women merely bore the children of men; the nineteenth-century view of women was that they merely played a supportive role for their husband's achievements and all the credit went to the men (the conventional Mrs Elvsted is all modesty as far as her own contribution to the book is concerned). There are also parallels in the treatment of the theme of jealousy—both Hedda and Medea pretend friendship to the rivals who have usurped their position, conceal their true feelings and plot destruction under the guise of friendship. Medea destroys Jason's new bride by giving her a coronet which burns into her golden hair. Hedda is jealous of Mrs Elvsted's beautiful hair. 'I think I shall burn your hair off, after all,' she says. Is this an accident, or an allusion, perhaps unconscious, to the earlier play? Medea is the daughter of a king, Hedda that of a general, and neither will suffer humiliation gladly. Medea says:

Yes, I can endure guilt, however horrible;
The laughter of my enemies I will not endure.

And Hedda prefers to take her own life rather than to endure social humiliation and the derisive laughter of Brack.

If a man grows tired
Of the company at home, he can go out, and find
A cure for tediousness. We wives are forced to look
To one man only. And, they tell us, we at home
Live free from danger. They go out to battle: fools!
I'd rather stand three times in the front line than bear
One child.

These lines are spoken by Medea, but could equally well have been spoken by Hedda, fretting in her drawing room, playing with her father's pistols, furious and disgusted with her own pregnant condition. Medea expatiates on the wretchedness of being born a woman. At one point she says:

We were born women—useless for honest purposes,
But in all kinds of evil skilled practitioners.

But in this case it is not yet another expression of woman as demon and monster, the alternative to woman as saint and angel—the two stereotypes of patriarchal drama—but a recognition on the part of Euripides that women are born with the same will and energy as men, which must become destructive if it cannot find a valid, constructive outlet. Ibsen also understood this. Women, he wrote, 'spend their lives inactively, dreaming and waiting for something unknown that will give their lives meaning. Their emotional lives are unhealthy as a consequence, and they become a prey to disillusion.'[1]

Both Ibsen and Euripides were exceptional for their time in seeing women as socially oppressed. Strindberg, with his paranoid hatred of the female sex, gave the old demonic tradition a new impetus. Shaw, as an enlightened socialist and feminist, and a great admirer of Ibsen, gave the misogyny of the idealist philosophers, Schopenhauer and Nietzsche in particular, a comic and less sinister turn by portraying woman as man's natural superior but glorying in it.

Whether or not Ibsen took *Medea* as a literary model for *Hedda Gabler*, the similarity was made possible because the position of women had changed so little during the intervening millennia. In the nineteenth century woman provided the last great tragic theme in the old style, because she was unique in still being hedged in with ancient taboos. In the novel, in particular, she constantly came to grief, usually by breaking her marriage vows in a moment of understandable weakness or folly, and respectable married ladies could quake in their boudoirs, moved by pity and terror, and resolve not to do likewise. Not only hack writers like Mrs Henry Wood, but great writers like Tolstoy and Flaubert could write convincingly on this theme, because the taboos still held their power. And gifted women writers like Charlotte Brontë and George Eliot were still held in its iron grip—Maggie Tulliver goes under, Jane Eyre cannot love without a wedding ring.

A male-dominated theatre in a patriarchal society will project masculine values and conflicts, just as history books, having been written by men, reflect male concerns: power, aggression, battles, victories, capital. The powerful females who figure in the history books from time to time seem to have something superhuman, almost monstrous about them (Boadicea, Catherine the Great, Elizabeth of England, Theodora) which suggests that, however admirable they may or may not have been in their way, they were somehow not quite 'normal' in their grip on the reins of power because they were women—if indeed, they were women. The suggestion that Elizabeth was a man in disguise or somehow physically abnormal is typical of the male reaction to any woman who shows herself capable of doing a 'man's job'.

History is a form of national mythology, and drama is one of the most fundamental ways of perpetuating that mythology. Even dramatists who are concerned with changing society, like

Brecht, make use of history. (Brecht was only too aware of the insidious power of presenting the past as a *fait accompli*, and his theory of alienation was an abortive attempt to get his audience to concentrate not on what is, but what should be.) So when women figure in patriarchal drama they play the roles assigned to them by a patriarchal society, as the wives or mothers of great men, or the love object. When, on occasion, they are shown as wielding power, they tend to assume the same monstrous qualities (superhuman and unfeminine) as they do in the history books. (The exceptions in the history books are also significant—thus Queen Victoria was always presented as a 'good' queen, one who left most political decision-making to her prime ministers, and went into lifelong mourning for her darling Albert who, during his lifetime, had been the decision-maker; a queen who also produced enough children to occupy most of the thrones of Europe.) In patriarchal drama women do not rule: they on occasion usurp power, and in doing so they show themselves monsters of depravity, schemers against men, and usually unchaste into the bargain.

Fifth-century Athens gave no civic or political rights to women. Sixteenth-century England experienced two ruling female monarchs, but only to safeguard a legitimate succession, and only after there were no direct male heirs available. Mary and Elizabeth were exceptions to the rule, and did not affect the common lot of women, which involved submission to their fathers or husbands. Indeed, Guevara, whose book was translated by Thomas North early in Elizabeth's reign, could have been inducement enough for her to avoid marriage, since he maintains that princesses and great ladies should obey their husbands, adding

> It is for aboundaunce of folly, and want of wisdome, that a woman should have presumption to governe a whole Realme, and that she hath not grace to obey one husband.

And the book makes clear that women are not really fit for high office:

> We see by experience that weomen of nature are all weake, fraile, fearful, & tender: and finally in matters of weight not very wise. Then if matters of government require not only science & experience, but also strength and courage to enterprise doubtfull things, wisedom for to know them, force to execute them, diligence for to followe them, pacience to suffer them, meanes to endure them, and above al great strength & hope to compasse them: why then will they take from man the governement, in whom al these things abounde, and geve it to the woman, in whom al these thinges doe wante. The ende why I speake these thinges before, is to require, to counsell, to admonishe, and to perswade Princesses and great Ladyes, that they thinke it spoken (if they wilbe happie in mariage) to thend they shoulde be obedient to their husbandes: for speaking the truth, in that house where the wife commaundeth the husbande, we may cal her a masculyne woman, and him a feminine man.

This is the situation we have in *Macbeth.* Macbeth may have masculine attributes of valour and ambition in the field, but he is not master in his own home. Lady Macbeth wishes for masculine attributes in herself and taunts her husband with his lack of masculinity. Significantly, the play was also written after the death of Elizabeth and the accession of James I, who disliked and distrusted women.

In male-dominated drama female roles will tend to fall into certain stereotypes, but it must also be remembered that the submission of women is part of a wider social and cosmic picture within which tragedy functioned. If people believed they had brought misfortune upon themselves by breaking a fundamental taboo, that taboo almost always involved observing certain social constraints, and for no one were the social constraints so clearly defined as for women. If men were responsible, ultimately, to the gods, women were answerable to their husbands or, if unmarried, to their fathers. So for women the first sin was lack of chastity, and even women in drama who break the rules by plotting for power are usually unchaste into the bargain. A man's honour involved his social obligations, a woman's honour was purely sexual. Later, with the emergence of the bourgeoisie, an honest man paid his debts, whilst an honest woman was faithful to her husband.

If recorded history tends to stereotype the sexes, dramatized history will take the process one step further, as dramatists and actors show heroes behaving heroically and women mourning their dead. Shakespeare created Lady Macbeth from a single line in Holinshed about Macbeth having an ambitious wife. In sixteenth-century England we can add the religious to the political sexual stereotypes: in the Christian religion all the teaching and proselytizing is done by men, and woman features as virgin, mother and contrite prostitute. She is there to suckle the babe and mourn the dead; to wash the feet of her master.

However much empathy a male dramatist may have for his female characters, the way he portrays his female characters will be limited by the very nature of the myths themselves, if he is working within a tradition of myth-perpetuating ideology. Euripides may give us a very pathetic Phaedra, but her ultimate destruction is inevitable. And his Andromache has all the conventional virtues:

> As Hector's wife I studied and practised the perfection of womanly modesty. I gave up all desire of visiting my neighbours and stayed in my own house—where a woman must stay, however blameless her reputation, unless she means to invite slander; and I refused to admit into my house the amusing gossip of other women. Having by nature a sound mind to school me, I was content; before my husband I kept a quiet tongue and a modest eye; I knew in what matters I should rule, and where I should yield to his authority.

The image of the perfect wife differs almost not at all from St Augustine's description, in the *Confessions*, of his perfect mother, who had also been a perfect wife:

> He was unfaithful to her, but her patience was so great that his infidelity never became a cause of quarrelling between

> them . . . he had a hot temper, but my mother knew better than to say or do anything to resist him when he was angry. If his anger was unreasonable, she used to wait until he was calm and composed and then took the opportunity of explaining what she had done. Many women, whose faces were disfigured by blows from husbands far sweeter tempered than her own, used to gossip together and complain of the behaviour of their men-folk. My mother would meet this complaint with another—about the women's tongues. Her manner was light but her meaning was serious when she told them that ever since they had heard the marriage read over them, they ought to have regarded it as a contract which bound them to serve their husbands, and from that time onward they should remember their condition and not defy their masters.

These two portraits give us an image which is the very reverse of Medea, who does not suffer ill-treatment on the part of her lord and master meekly and without resentment, but instead lashes back at him, both with her tongue and with terrible actions. Patience is a virtue particularly required of women in patriarchal drama, and the patient Grizelda figure is particularly popular in Christian literature and drama. She is unjustly accused by her lord, usually of infidelity, is banished, incarcerated or otherwise abandoned or maltreated,but waits patiently and uncomplainingly for her innocence to be revealed, not through her own efforts, but the fullness of time. And the good woman also tends to be a silent one. She does not scold or nag, and she does not gossip with other women. Many sermons were preached against the wagging tongues of women. Cordelia bears traces of the ideal woman of medieval legend: she is monosyllabic where her sisters are fulsome, she is unjustly accused and banished but suffers in silence, and her voice was, as Lear remembers when she is dead, 'ever soft,/Gentle and low, an excellent thing in woman'. But she is of course far from being a negative character. Silence and the capacity to endure can become symptoms of strength.

Because patriarchy requires women to be submissive, to suffer cruelty and injustice without attempting to retaliate, the good women in tragedy also tend to become the pathetic victims. They are rejected by the men they love and pine away, they are unjustly accused of infidelity and are murdered in a fit of rage—and the irate husband or lover discovers the truth too late. Ophelia and Desdemona belong to this genre. The same situations are set up in comedy, but here everything ends well and the misunderstanding or deception is discovered without irreparable damage having been done—Hero is not dead, the statue of Hermione comes to life and she returns to the arms of her repentant husband. It is however important to remember that the pathos of the unhappy ending, and the reunion of the happy ending depends on the innocence of the woman, her total fidelity and chastity. *Othello* is a tragedy, not because it shows us a man killing his wife, but because a man kills his *innocent* wife. He has been wickedly deceived by a lying schemer and finds out his error too late. There were contemporary dramas which showed husbands killing wives who had committed adultery, and the audiences were not expected to shed tears, merely to enjoy the horrific spectacle. It is significant that adultery was added to the other crimes of Goneril and Regan, and that when their corpses are brought in this is the fact of which the audience is reminded, and it is their adulterous passion which brought about their deaths. The comment on the bodies is made by Edmund:

> *Yet Edmund was belov'd:*
> *The one the other poison'd for my sake,*
> *And after slew herself.*

The contrast between Goneril and Regan on the one hand, and Cordelia on the other, is total. It is not a question of degree, or shades of grey, but of black and white, total goodness and total evil. This is a tendency in patriarchal drama, since men cannot forgive frailty in women. Since the image of woman relates to the demands made upon her by an all-powerful male, she is seen as either totally good or totally bad, all innocence and purity, or completely evil, lascivious and scheming. She is not seen as a human being, with understandable faults and frailties, a weak person who may grow strong in the course of the drama. A man may grow and change in the course of a play, his frailties may cause him suffering but also give him a new wisdom. But women do not become, they simply *are*. Lear changes and grows, but Cordelia is always the same figure of steadfast goodness. Regan and Goneril die as wickedly as they have lived, without apparently having learned anything. Macbeth grows in stature even as he grows in wickedness, whilst his wife simply cracks as the weak vessel, when she first seemed so strong. Hamlet and Othello also grow in stature, while their women die as they have lived, small and frail and vulnerable. And to go back much, much further: Oedipus survives, broken and mutilated, to become a figure of sanctity, but Jocasta dies. No woman who has known sin, who has once been stained, can ever be acceptable—she is a damaged vessel which must be destroyed.

The wicked woman in patriarchal drama is guilty of two main offences: she is sexually unchaste and she tries to usurp the male prerogative of power. And since the male image of woman tends to fall into extremes of black and white, since the essence of a good woman is in her womanliness (as defined by men), the two forms of female wickedness tend to combine in the same character. Clytemnestra takes a lover in her husband's absence and on his return they conspire to murder the husband and thus take over his kingdom. In the text of Aeschylus she is constantly referred to as manlike. 'I am the man to speak', she says, on her first entrance, and although this might sound like a compliment, within patriarchal terms it is in fact the opposite, implies usurpation, a monstrosity of nature. Lady Macbeth, who is also interested in power, also 'unsexes' herself. In contrast to the meek Lady Macduff, who is shown as a pathetic victim, portrayed as a tender mother, Lady Macbeth swears herself ready to dash her suckling baby's brains out rather than fail in her resolve. But however monstrous the two women may be, they cannot ultimately destroy the male-dominated hierarchy, even though they represent a serious threat. 'Help! Look, a nightmare! What? will cow gore bull?' exclaims Cassandra, but ultimately the monster is destroyed, as she must be, just as Lady

Macbeth cracks first because she is, in spite of her claims to manhood, only a woman.

It is interesting to compare Clytemnestra and Lady Macbeth, both powerful figures who seem somewhat larger than life. Both are referred to, and refer to themselves, as manlike, both appear very bold but are ultimately haunted by supernatural dreams, and both plot with their menfolk to commit murder, but rely on the man to do the actual deed. Each boasts about her strong nerves in the face of murder. 'You speak as to some thoughtless woman: you are wrong./My pulse beats firm'—thus Clytemnestra to the chorus after the murder of Agamemnon. Lady Macbeth constantly upbraids her husband for not being man enough ('When you durst do it then you were a man'), boasts that she is more of a man than he is, and declares in a matter-of-fact tone after the murder that 'A little water clears us of this deed'. But the whole long cycle of the *Oresteia* finally turns on the need to re-establish the desired order of society, whereby men should rule over women. It is not just that a murder has been committed, because there have been many murders—it is that a woman has conspired to murder her lord and master. 'Female shall murder male: what kind of brazenness/Is that?' exclaims Cassandra, and the chorus upbraids Clytemnestra:

> *Vile woman! What unnatural food or drink,*
> *Malignant root, brine from the restless sea*
> *Transformed you, that your nature did not shrink*
> *From foulest guilt?*

She has become a monster not just because murder is monstrous, but because for a woman to do such a deed against a man is doubly monstrous. The doctor who sees Lady Macbeth sleepwalk refers to the incident as 'a great perturbation in nature', and this has more than a psychological meaning. Lady Macbeth has behaved in an 'unnatural' way, not only because regicide is an offence against the natural order, but because she has gone against her own womanly nature. Early in the play she was conscious of what she was doing:

Come, you spirits
That tend on mortal thoughts! unsex me here,
And fill me from the crown to the toe top full
Of direst cruelty; make thick my blood
Stop up the access and passage to remorse,
That no compunctious visitings of nature
Shake my fell purpose, nor keep peace between
The effect and it! Come to my woman's breasts,
And take my milk for gall, you murdering ministers . . .

The perturbations of an unnatural woman are reflected in the rest of nature, chaos is come again when a king is killed by his subject and a woman goes against her gentle and unassuming nature. 'What? will cow gore bull?' exclaims Cassandra as she sees the events that are about to take place. After the murder of Duncan an old man recalls that

On Tuesday last,
A falcon, towering in her pride of place,
Was by a mousing owl hawk'd at and kill'd.

And Ross recalls that Duncan's horses had broken free and eaten each other.

In the *Oresteia* of Aeschylus, it is interesting that Clytemnestra should have such a commanding position in the drama, particularly when you consider that the story concerns a whole chain of murders. But earlier events are not shown. We do not, for instance, see the conflict between Agamemnon and his wife over the sacrifice of their daughter. This would have made a very dramatic first play for a trilogy, but would also have shifted sympathy towards Clytemnestra. Instead we are shown a triumphant king and hero brutally murdered on his return from the war. Lady Macbeth also assumes a very commanding position in Shakespeare's play, which is particularly interesting in view of the fact that Holinshed's only reference to her in his chronicles is the brief line to the effect that Macbeth's wife 'lay sore upon him to attempt the thing', she being 'very ambitious brenning in unquenchable desire to bear the name of Queen'.

One can see that such a line, however brief, could fire the imagination of a dramatist, but the dominant position of the figure of Lady Macbeth in this particular play is interesting for other reasons.

Macbeth is a Scottish history play written to please a new patron who had recently ascended the English throne. James I was known to believe in witches, had written a book on demonology, and had tended to reverse any progress towards enlightenment on this subject. For instance, he ordered Reginald Scot's book, which took a mocking and sceptical attitude to the existence of witches, to be publicly burned. The witches in Shakespeare's play suffer a transformation from the figures that appear in Holinshed's chronicle. Holinshed had described them as 'women in strange and ferly apparel, resembling creatures of an elder world . . . Goddesses of destiny, or else some nymphs or fairies, endowed with knowledge of prophecy by their necromantical science'. But there is nothing nymph-like about the women in the play, they are the horrible crones of popular belief. And it is in this particular play, where witches and witchcraft figures so largely, that we also have the dominating figure of Lady Macbeth. Apart from the witches and Lady Macbeth, the only other female character (apart from the gentlewoman of the sleepwalking scene) is Lady Macduff who, as we have already said, provides a contrast to Lady Macbeth. Lady Macbeth is never shown with her children, all we know is that she is prepared to dash her baby's brains out if the need arises, but we also know that she was a mother. But she is never shown in a maternal role which might arouse sympathy, just as Clytemnestra is never shown in relation to Iphigenia. In addition there is something distinctly witchlike about Lady Macbeth herself. On her very first entrance she addresses unseen spirits. She seems peculiarly unafraid of supernatural manifestations, when the contemporary attitude was that good Christians ought to beware. Is she a sceptic like Edmund in *King Lear*, or is she in cahoots with the Devil? We obviously choose the first interpretation, but it is more than possible that many of Shakespeare's original audience, particularly the more superstitious amongst them, chose the second. Certainly James I, his most eminent patron, would have chosen the second. It must be remembered that a strong belief in witchcraft involves a fear and hatred of women, *all* women, and particularly of their demonic power. That demonic power is sexual. The real hold of Lady Macbeth over her husband is sexual; when she taunts him about his manhood it is not only a reference to his prowess as a soldier, but to his prowess in the bedroom. James I would have been familiar with the *Malleus Maleficarum*, the standard textbook on witchcraft, which makes it clear that all women are liable to be in league with the Devil, and that their evil power is a sexual one; and it is more than likely that Shakespeare did his homework on the subject before embarking on a play to please his master, whose beliefs on women and witches were well known.

Women were supposed to stand in a relationship of loving obedience to two male authority figures—the husband, and the father. Before the murder of Duncan Lady Macbeth only hesitates once, but it is a significant hesitation:

> *Had he not resembled*
> *My father as he slept I had done't.*

It is a curious admission of weakness in one who has appeared so ruthless and determined. We can perhaps see it as the first inkling that Lady Macbeth is no monster but simply a human being, and a woman at that. Certainly Regan, who *is* described as a monster after the scene, has no such scruples when Gloucester's eyes are put out. But after the deed is done Lady Macbeth behaves with great sang-froid; she does not, for instance, faint at the sight of blood, which makes her later fit of fainting an obvious deception—in company she behaves in the way that a woman is supposed to do. Even though she is ruthless and dominates over her husband, something holds her back when Duncan resembles her father in sleep.

In a patriarchal society a daughter's obedience to her father is absolute. Her father makes the ultimate decision as to whom she shall marry, and as a result many dramas hinge on the fact. Juliet and Desdemona both marry against their father's wishes and die for it. In *A Midsummer Night's Dream* a father demands the death penalty for his daughter if she will not marry the man of his choice; the daughter, who has chosen another man, runs away. Because it is a comedy everything ends happily, the daughter marries the man she loves and the rejected suitor is—with the help of a little magic—induced to fall in love with her previously rejected friend. The father has no alternative but to concur in the new arrangement. But the beginning of the play is serious enough, just as the charge of Claudio against Hero could not be more serious in *Much Ado*. Even though the stories might be set in exotic countries, the morals were contemporary and English. A contemporary audience would have been scandalized at the imputation that a girl of good family was not a virgin on her wedding day, and such a charge could not but be of the highest seriousness. If true, a girl was ruined, in which case she was probably better off dead; if not true, Claudio's mistake was a disastrous and cruel one. If the innocent Hero had really died, we would have had another tragedy like *Othello*, with the male hero deceived into believing slander by a machiavell.

Shakespeare seems to have been somewhat obsessed with the relationship between fathers and daughters. Just as Lady Macbeth's hesitation shows her to be human, and a woman after all, Cressida puts herself beyond the pale when she declares 'I have forgot my father'. Lear puts his curse on the wrong daughter and she ultimately dies. Ophelia, who is an obedient daughter, in a sense dies because her father misjudges the situation and instructs her in a misguided fashion.

In comedy the conflict between fathers and daughters is a straight one about marriage choices and the outcome is happy. Hermia elopes with impunity even though Theseus had told her that 'To you, your father should be as a god'. Jessica also runs away, and in her case there is no question of remonstrance since her father is a Jew. Imogen in *Cymbeline* not only marries against her father's wishes but is slandered on the question of her chaste fidelity into the bargain, but all ends happily. The conflict between daughter's wishes and paternal authority is ideally resolved in *The Tempest*, where the daughter is brought up on a remote and secluded island where she has never seen any man other than her father; who, being a magician, magically draws the approved suitor to its shores at the desired moment. Thus family conflict is removed, the father remains in control of his daughter, who has no cause to rebel, but is happy and grateful in her sheltered innocence.

The first requirement of a wife or prospective wife in patriarchal drama is chastity, with obedience coming a close second. Phaedra only lusted after her stepson, and the intention is enough to fill her with guilt and shame; in the comic fragment of *The Samian Woman* the main character is suspected of very similar behaviour by her husband but, as is usual in comedy, the woman is found to be blameless 'after all'. So that the audience should know how to react to the situation there is usually no doubt: they know from the start that Hero and Desdemona are blameless, so that they become pathetic figures worthy of sympathy. In the tragedy Desdemona is really dead, in the comedy the bride survives to marry her bridegroom. The modern reaction would surely be that Hero should not have married a man who could insult her so cruelly; but that is not the point at issue within this framework of ethics—the man had been given false information and his behaviour was therefore justifiable. In Chapman's *Bussy d'Ambois* there is a scene between a jealous husband and his wife which is reminiscent of *Othello*, except that in this case the wife *is* guilty of adultery. Thus the torments to which Montsurry subjects Tamyra are entirely justified by the situation: he stabs her a couple of times, then puts her on the rack to discover the name of her lover and that of the go-between. There is no suggestion that his behaviour is in any way reprehensible. In *Othello* there is a suggestion that the tragedy has to some extent been brought about for ethnic reasons, that no European nobleman (the kind of man her father would have wanted her to marry) would have been so gullible or hot-blooded. Othello is strong and brave but he is also an innocent, unused to the machiavellian intrigues of Italian courts. In this sense Desdemona brings her doom on herself, by her initial disobedience. In Cinthio's original story Desdemona says: 'Nay, but you Moors are of so hot a nature, that every little trifle moves you to anger and revenge', and later she declares: 'much I fear, that I shall prove a warning to young girls not to marry against the wishes of their parents, and that the Italian ladies may learn from me not to wed a man whom nature and habitude of life estrange from us'. The situation is heightened in the drama by Desdemona's very obvious innocence—obvious to the audience, but not to Othello. She is so pure, so childlike, that the gullibility of Othello seems greater, although the drama does of course basically function within the convention of innocence maligned by the machiavell.

An Italian lady who does obey her father's instructions about marriage, even though he is dead, is Portia, though she cheats a little by giving her favourite man helpful clues during the guessing game. At first glance Portia appears to play a very male role, but she does in fact embody the positive aspects of woman in patriarchal drama. The good woman in Greek drama could be portrayed as an embodiment of strength, quiet endurance and even courage. Later there was a tendency for the good woman to embody all the specifically Christian virtues, since Christianity preaches the virtues of meekness, mildness and mercy, which were regarded as desirable feminine qualities. (Later Nietzsche was to regard Christianity as feminine in a pejorative sense.) Thus Portia plays advocate for the Christian viewpoint in a play which hinges on an argument between supposedly Judaic ethic and the Christian ethic, between strict justice and mercy, between capitalism and usury on the one hand and the concept of friendship and charity on the other.

Men wield power, and power usually has little time for the Christian virtues, whether the power is exercised in the political or economic sphere; it is therefore left to women to remind men that it behoves men to temper justice with mercy. Portia's famous speech on the quality of mercy is matched by similar speeches in other plays of the period which are spoken by women. In Tourneur's *The Atheist's Tragedy* the chaste Castabella pleads:

> *O father, mercy is an attribute*
> *As high as justice, an essential part*
> *Of his unbounded goodness, whose divine*
> *Impression, form, and image man should bear.*

And methinks man should love to imitate
His mercy, since the only countenance
Of justice were destruction, if the sweet
And loving favour of his mercy did
Not mediate between it and our weakness.

The message is overtly Christian, in a play which concerns an atheist. In *Measure for Measure* (which is another way of saying 'an eye for an eye'), it is the virtuous and chaste Isabella who makes a similar plea for justice to be tempered with mercy:

No ceremony that to great ones 'longs,
Not the king's crown, nor the deputed sword,
The marshal's truncheon, nor the judge's robe,
Become them with one half so good a grace
As mercy does.

When Angelo refuses to listen, declaring that her brother is forfeit to the law, her pleading becomes more specifically Christian:

Why, all the souls that were were forfeit once;
And He that might the vantage best have took,
Found out the remedy. How would you be,
If He, which is the top of judgement, should
But judge you as you are?

This reference to the role of Christ as the Redeemer of sinners, which all men are, is in this case also prophetic, since Isabella will, in the last scene, kneel to plead for Angelo himself. Since *Coriolanus* takes place in a non-Christian society Shakespeare cannot make use of such a plea when Volumnia kneels to her son, together with his wife. So the Roman matron confines herself to reproaching him with the words:

Think'st thou it honourable for a noble man
Still to remember wrongs?

This immediately after comparing him to a god in his aspirations. Since the gods in question are Roman she cannot go on to speak of divine mercy, and confines herself to reminding him that the thunderbolts of the gods only split oak trees, and do not destroy states. She also accuses him of having more pride than pity, and suggests that the gods may punish him for not allowing her to fulfil her duty. This is as far as the lady can go, given her pagan situation. Except in one respect: a Christian lady can kneel and plead and have holy dignity in that position, but as a Roman matron she can play on her son's embarrassment by kneeling to him, when he owes her honour, as his mother.

The Christian qualities of mercy which these heroines voice emphasize a very particular aspect of women in a patriarchal society. In his book *The Ritual Process* Victor Turner explores the antithesis between 'structure' and 'communitas' in a society, and points out that in closed or structured societies it is the person of low status who tends to symbolize communitas:

> Where patrilineality is the basis of the social structure, an individual's link to other members of his society through the mother, and hence by extension and abstraction 'women' and 'femininity', tends to symbolize that wider community and its ethical system that encompasses and pervades the politico-legal system.[2]

In a society where men wield power it is left to women to remind men with power that we are all brothers under the skin, all children of God.

Male drama, written and performed by men, always carries an implicit comment on the nature and conduct of women. But because the stage is dominated by men explicit comment is also usual. The audiences are treated to generalizations on the nature and weaknesses of women whilst men as a sex are never subjected to such comment. Men's weaknesses and foibles may be remarked on, particular vices may be diagnosed, but men as an entire sex, a race almost, are not the subject of generalized comment. Often the comment on women is intended to invite jeering laughter from the audience, and it is always intended to reinforce existing prejudices. Mostly the comments are derogatory and elicit a stock response (like jokes about mothers-in-law or women drivers in our own century), but at times the comments are idealized when woman is seen as the object of idealized love.

The English tradition in this respect goes right back to the Middle Ages, when Church clerics made a habit of castigating the female sex from the pulpit and in the written word. This was in line with a long tradition of accepted doctrine, since woman was responsible for all the sins in the world. The pulpit was also the place where the social mores were most effectively reinforced, where it could be brought home to the silent female congregation that it behoved them to obey their husbands, and that vanity or wagging tongues would surely lead to eternal damnation. And men would come out of church with their own feelings of superiority and righteous authority reinforced. No Christian woman would quarrel with the good book, which was full of quotations on the iniquities of the female sex, and hell fire awaited those who dared to disagree. Long before hell fire, however, there were punishments of a painful sort in this world.

So the habit of commenting unfavourably on the female sex in general has its roots in patriarchy and its official licence in the Christian Church. In the Wakefield mystery cycle there is a good early example. Typically, the diatribe is out of all proportion to the provocation, although the speaker is, appropriately, St Paul. Mary Magdalene claims to have met the risen Christ but St Paul does not trust her:

And it is written in our law
No woman's judgement hold in awe,
Nor too quickly show belief:
For with their cunning and their guile
They can laugh then weep awhile,
When nothing gives them grief.

In our books thus find we written,
All manner of men have so been bitten,
By women in this wise:
Like an apple ripe is she,
A joy, without a doubt to see,
On the board as it lies.

If any take and start to chew
It is rotten through and through
To the core within:
Wherefore in woman is no law,
For she holds nothing in awe,
As Christ me save from sin.

Therefore we trust not easily,
Unless we saw it surely,
And in the manner how:
In woman's word trust have we nought,
For they are fickle in word and thought,
To that I make my vow.

Just as the words of St Paul could be used to castigate women in church, to keep them in their position of lowly subjection, so St Paul as a character on stage becomes a good excuse for a lengthy diatribe on the wickedness of women. The fact that Mary Magdalene is right in her assertion is beside the point, is almost totally forgotten by dramatist and audience as the action stops for a lecture on the cunning wiles and deceitfulness of woman. Woman, please note, is no longer just the person who handed man the apple, she is the apple, the rotten apple which is fair without and foul within. This is also part of the Christian tradition: since woman is sexually beguiling, men have to be doubly on their guard. In the Scriptures and in other religious texts men are constantly warned that woman may be fair without but that she is a foul danger underneath. Under that fair exterior lurks a serpent, a sewer, a cesspool of foulness. This is a tradition which continues into secular drama, as we shall see, and finds strong expression there.

One might, I suppose, argue that the above verse is spoken by St Paul, and that this is dramatically justified by the known views of that apostle. But such comments occur elsewhere in the text. The demons in 'The Judgment' of the Wakefield cycle make derogatory remarks on 'the feminine gender', and a character called Tutivillus comments on women's capacity to lead men astray in terms that echo the words of St Paul but are at the same time unmistakably secular and contemporary:

So jolly
Each lass in the land
Ladylike here at hand,
So fresh none may withstand,
Leads men to folly

If she be never so foul a dowd, with her nets and her pins,
The shrew herself can shroud, both her cheeks and her chins;
She can caper full proud with japes and with gins,
Her head high in a cloud, but not shamed by her sins
Or evil;
With this powder and paint,
She plans to look quaint,
She may smile like a saint,
But at heart is a devil.

Woman as a devil who looks like an angel is a familiar theme in Christian literature. It is strong in sixteenth-century drama, where it has its roots in Christian doctrine, supported by apt quotations from the Bible. Later the theme was revived in more legendary guise by the Romantics, in 'La Belle Dame Sans Merci', for instance. But for Shakespeare's contemporaries the idea had its firm roots not in dim and distant legend, but in an immediate moral order. Woman represented temptation, mortal sin, the Devil in disguise. Desdemona is an angel, looks like an angel, but bears a devilish name, and Emilia calls Othello the blacker devil for making a mistake. The idea of the woman who is a devil and looks like an angel recurs again and again in the drama of the period. The fact that these women were played by boys, bewigged and painted, must have reinforced the concept. So when Hamlet says

> I have heard of your paintings too, well enough; God hath given you one face, and you make yourselves another: you jig, you amble, and you lisp, and nickname God's creatures, and make your wantonness your ignorance. Go to, I'll no more on't . . .

he is not only echoing the pulpit admonitions against female vanity and artfulness, but speaking to an actor who really has painted on another face, who really does lisp and trip in imitation of something he is not. The fact that the lovely young girl is performed by a male can help to underline the idea that a woman is what she is not, that she pretends in order to beguile men, that the fair exterior is false, as the apple with its tempting exterior in the Wakefield cycle is in fact rotten to the core.

The strongest expression of the Christian image of woman as diabolical is in *King Lear*, and it is a speech which brings out very clearly the sexual connotations which are fundamental to Christian belief. Sex is sin, woman represents the temptation to sin, therefore woman is the Devil, or his agent:

> *Down from the waist they are Centaurs,*
> *Though women all above:*
> *But to the girdles do the gods inherit,*
> *Beneath is all the fiends':*
> *There's hell, there's darkness, there's the sulphurous pit,*
> *Burning, scalding, stench, consumption; fie, fie, fie!*

Lear is supposed to be a pagan king, so the reference to 'the gods' is overtly pagan; otherwise the imagery and the sentiments are unmistakably Christian; it may start with centaurs, but it finishes with a Christian depiction of Hell. And what is really interesting about this passage is that the woman's sexual organ has become Hell itself, and that the last two lines express strong sexual disgust. The disgust is strengthened by a distinct reference to venereal disease in the words 'burning, scalding, stench, consumption'.

I am not trying to imply that Shakespeare was a misogynist, merely that he was working within a tradition. Speeches which express such a view are contained within the dramatic action, spoken—for instance—by a lover who believes himself to be deceived and who may well be mistaken, as Hamlet appears to be mistaken about Ophelia, though his distrust of her may be part of his pretended madness. He certainly tests her possibly rotten and lascivious interior: 'Lady, shall I lie in your lap?' The trouble about being truly chaste and virtuous is that even *double-entendres* of this kind should be beyond a maiden's comprehension. Other female characters in Shakespeare's plays indulge freely in sexual banter without anyone being expected to think the worse of them for that, but Ophelia's virtue, since it is in question, and since a dominant theme in the play is that of semblance and reality, must be made clear, so she either does not understand or she does not react at all to Hamlet's sexual innuendoes:

> Hamlet: *Do you think I meant country matters?*
> Ophelia: *I think nothing, my lord.*
> Hamlet: *That's a fair thought to lie between maids' legs.*
> Ophelia: *What is, my lord?*

Is she really so innocent, or is she merely playing the innocent? This is an important question for Hamlet who has, because of his mother's conduct, recently been led to view women with a jaundiced eye. 'Frailty, thy name is woman!' he had commented early on, thus reiterating an accepted Christian doctrine. Woman is the weaker vessel, and thus more open to sin. The ghost refers to Gertrude as 'my most seeming-virtuous queen', with the emphasis, obviously, on 'seeming'. She is an example of woman with a fair exterior who is rotten within.

Within this system of values the tragedy is not only that men can be beguiled by a bad woman, but that they can also make mistakes about a truly good one, seeing guile where there is none, as Othello does in the case of Desdemona, and as Hamlet would *appear* to do in the case of Ophelia. Hero, like Desdemona, is the victim of a slanderous plot against her honour, and when Claudio rejects her he does so by appealing to the audience in terms which they would have understood and approved:

She's but the sign and semblance of her honour.
Behold! how like a maid she blushes here.
O! what authority and show of truth
Can cunning sin cover itself withal.
Comes not that blood as modest evidence
To witness simple virtue? Would you not swear,
All you that see her, that she were a maid,
By these exterior shows? But she is none:
She knows the heat of a luxurious bed;
Her blush is guiltiness, not modesty.

We have dramatic irony here, in that the audience knows Hero to be innocent, that her blush really is one of outraged modesty and innocence; but at the same time a contemporary audience would have sympathized with Claudio in his position, just as they would have done with that of Othello, since women were deceitful and deceiving creatures, in the habit of dissembling virtues they were far from practising. A modern audience may find Claudio very unsympathetic, unworthy of forgiveness, but a contemporary audience would have sympathized with his dilemma: one ought to be wary of the goods one is purchasing.

In comedy men are given a second chance which—no one questions—they really deserve. Hero is alive, not dead, and returns to marry her bridegroom. The wife of Leontes, also publicly denounced as unfaithful, steps down from her pedestal, a statue come back to life, a full sixteen years later to be embraced and taken back by a husband she never deceived. And Posthumus is also given a second chance after his innocent wife had supposedly been murdered at his command for her supposed infidelity. When Posthumus believes himself betrayed he delivers a speech which sums up the patriarchal attitude to women at its most extreme, whereby woman is made responsible for all the sins in the world:

Could I find out
The woman's part in me! For there's no motion
That tends to vice in man but I affirm
It is the woman's part; be it lying, note it,
The woman's; flattering, hers; deceiving, hers;
Lust and rank thoughts, hers, hers; revenges, hers;
Ambitions, covetings, change of prides, disdain,
Nice longing, slanders, mutability,
All faults that man may name, nay, that hell knows,
Why, hers, in part, or all; but rather, all;
For even to vice
They are not constant, but are changing still . . .

This is an orthodox opinion which would have inclined the audience to sympathize with the speaker, who would then not have been inclined to question his right to have his wife murdered, or Imogen's constancy and devotion in spite of such treatment. A man has a difficult time where women are concerned, since it is so hard to tell black from white, and if he makes a mistake he is to be pitied rather than condemned. In *Cymbeline* the innocence of Imogen is contrasted with the wickedness of her stepmother and, just as Posthumus can be excused for mistaking virtue for vice, so Cymbeline excuses himself for mistaking vice for virtue. 'Who is't can read a woman?' he exclaims, and he goes on:

Mine eyes
Were not in fault, for she was beautiful;
Mine ears, that heard her flattery; nor my heart,
That thought her like her seeming:

The senses are the doors to sin and wicked witches and women, as Jacob Sprenger, the famous inquisitor of witches in the fifteenth century, had pointed out so repetitively in *Malleus Maleficarum*, attack the virtue of men through their senses. 'The power of the devil lies in the privy parts of men,' he wrote, for 'although the devil cannot directly operate upon the understanding and will of man, yet . . . he can act upon the body, or upon the faculties belonging to or allied to the body.' Naturally woman would not be such a snare if she did not have such a fair exterior. 'Fair is foul, and foul is fair,' say the witches in *Macbeth.* How is a poor, ordinary mortal man to know one from the other? No wonder so much drama is concerned with his dilemma.

Wicked stepmothers are of course by no means confined to the play *Cymbeline.* The contrast between young innocence and the depravity and corruption of an older woman features quite often in plays of the period and has also passed into folklore. We have this contrast between Gertrude and Ophelia in *Hamlet.* Cordelia is the youngest daughter. Older women have learned in the school of life to be cunning and devious, they know how to use their sex, in contrast to the innocent young virgin, to manipulate men; if they are the wives or, better still, the widows of powerful men, they can themselves wield power.

Tourneur, who is much concerned with corruption at court, depicts the corruption of women in terms of chastity, and makes a very sharp division between those women who are chaste and those who are not. Both *The Atheist's Tragedy* and *The Revenger's Tragedy* feature corrupt older women, unbridled in their lust, who are contrasted with the virtuous and chaste daughters they are quite prepared to see dishonoured at a price. These older women try, without success, to convert their chaste daughters to a philosophy of expediency and social advancement through sex. They are the female equivalent of the male 'politician', who seeks advancement by fair means or foul, who is devious and cunning and whose only moral law is not to be found out. These older women not only try to corrupt their virgin daughters, but deceive their own husbands with alacrity. The text of both plays is littered with sour generalities on the nature of women, though to be fair Tourneur is not exactly enchanted with men either. In *The Revenger's Tragedy* we are given a medieval emblem of the good woman: ie., the chaste wife. Antonio's wife has killed herself after being ravished, not wishing to live dishonoured. (This might seem to us to be taking things a bit far, but since woman is an object her will does not come into it—her husband's possession has been spoilt and so the virtuous wife does away with herself, thus relieving her husband of an embarrassment.) The corpse is revealed to the audience, and described by her grieving husband:

> *A prayer-book the pillow to her cheek;*
> *This was her rich confection, and another*
> *Plac'd in her right hand, with a leaf tuck'd up,*
> *Pointing to these words:*
> Melius virtute mori, quam per dedecus vivere.

The message is made explicit, and this pious wife is shown as a moral example to the audience, and to all women. As the bearer of a man's children a woman is judged by her actual chastity, not her emotions or intentions. Having been raped, Antonio's wife knew the honourable course to take, and thus became a shining and, indeed, tragic example for other women.

The dishonest male tries to seek social advancement by scheming in these plays, whilst the dishonest woman tries to better herself through sex. When Vindice in *The Revenger's Tragedy* disguises himself and tries to tempt his virtuous sister, he says: 'Why are there so few honest women, but because 'tis the poorer profession?' but when he reveals his true identity to his curiously unobservant mother he chides her, as Hamlet chides his sinful mother, and he gives the age-old Christian view of women as the corrupters of men:

> *Were't not for gold and women, there would be no*
> *damnation: Hell would look like a lord's great*
> *kitchen without fire in't:*
> *But 'twas decreed before the world began,*
> *That they should be the hooks to catch at man.*

'All witchcraft comes from carnal lust, which is in women insatiable,' wrote Sprenger, and the character Ambitioso voices the same sentiment in Tourneur's play:

> *Most women have small waists the world throughout,*
> *But their desires are thousand miles about.*

But because women are the weaker vessels both the villainesses, Levidulcia and Gratiana, are shown repentant at the end: they are swayed by their lust rather than by any firm purpose. In fact Levidulcia, at the end of *The Atheist's Tragedy*, kills herself and thus provides an equivalent of the example given by the death of Antonio's wife in *The Revenger's Tragedy*. In this case she herself speaks the moral:

> *Shall I outlive my honour? Must my life*
> *Be made the world's example? Since it must,*
> *Then thus in detestation of my deed,*
> *To make th' example move more forcibly*
> *To virtue, thus I seal it with a death*
> *As full of horror as my life.* [stabs herself]

Women in the audience, take note.

In *Bussy d'Ambois* we have a similar parallel between unscrupulous scheming on the part of men and adultery on the part of women. But whilst Bussy has all the daring and assurance of Edmund in *King Lear*, Tamyra is less certain about the rights and wrongs of her behaviour. The text is peppered with generalities about the fickleness, deception and frailty of the female soul, but like Tourneur's villainess and Lady Macbeth, Tamyra is not even steadfast in wickedness. Bussy tries to encourage her in her wickedness by scoffing at conscience and cowardly superstition, but his scepticism, like that of Edmund, has to be vanquished in the end. Tamyra is tortured and put to death in full view of the audience—no doubt to their horrified delight—and given a certain tragic pathos by her obvious repentance and humility.

The generalities on the nature of women in *Bussy d'Ambois* will by now have a familiar ring to the reader:

> *Urge reason to them, it will do no good;*
> *Humour (that is the chariot of our food*
> *In every body) must in them be fed,*
> *To carry their affections by it bred.* (Friar)

O the infinite regions betwixt a woman's tongue and her heart. (Monsieur)

O the unsound Sea of women's bloods,
That when 'tis calmest, is most dangerous . . .

Not Cerberus ever saw the damned nooks
Hid with the veils of women's virtuous looks . . . (Monsieur)

Again the contrast between semblance and reality, apparent virtue and hidden vice. 'Woman,' wrote Sprenger, 'is a wheedling and secret enemy'

> And that she is more perilous than a snare does not speak of the snare of hunters, but of devils. For men are caught not only through their carnal desires, when they see and hear women: for S. Bernard says: Their face is as a burning wind, and their voice the hissing of serpents . . . And when it is said that her heart is a net, it speaks of the inscrutable malice which reigns in their hearts.

This description is almost paraphrased in *Bussy*:

The errant wilderness of a woman's face;
Where men cannot get out, for all the Comets
That have been lighted at it; though they know
That Adders lie a-sunning in their smiles,
That Basilisks drink their poison from their eyes,
And no way there to coast out to their hearts; (Montsurry)

Eve, who gave Adam the apple, herself becomes the rotten apple. Now she has also become the serpent. The friar in this play, who is presumably not vulnerable to female sexual wiles, takes a more scholastic view of the sex.

In Marston's play *The Insatiate Countess* we also get the view that women are responsible for all the sins of men, in a speech given authority by a doctrinal touch from the medieval schoolmen:

Man were on earth an angel but for woman,
That seven-fold branch of hell from them doth grow,
Pride, lust, and murder, they raise from below,
With all their fellow-sins. Women are made
Of blood, without souls;

And the same speaker voices the idea that men are bewitched by devils who look like angels:

Thou dotest upon a devil, not a woman,
That has bewitcht thee with her sorcery,
And drown'd thy soul in leathy faculties.
Her useless lust has benumb'd thy knowledge;
Thy intellectual powers, oblivion smothers,
That thou art nothing but forgetfulness.

Man's rational faculty is undermined by the physicality (devoid of mind or soul) of women. Mind belongs to God but flesh and the sins thereof do, of course, belong to the Devil. And women driven by an adulterous appetite will not even stop at murder (Goneril and Regan are examples of such monsters in human form):

This curse pursues female adultery,
They'll swim through blood for sin's variety;
Their pleasure like a sea, groundless and wide,
A woman's lust was never satisfied.

Like Levidulcia in *The Atheist's Tragedy*, the insatiate countess dies as a self-conscious example to other women. When her husband comes to visit her on the scaffold she exclaims:

O, my offended lord, lift up your eyes:
But yet avert them from my loathed sight.
Had I with you enjoyed the lawful pleasure,
To which belongs nor fear nor public shame,
I might have liv'd in honour, died in fame!

As the more pliable sex, female characters are more liable to show remorse in extremity, which is also convenient for internalizing the moral. Since the character has herself recognized the error of her ways, the audience will be even less prone to question the moral.

Women were considered more pliable, more prone to weakness, which justified man's control over them. It was necessary for men to have authority over women for the same reason that it was necessary for parents to have authority over children. Helen and Cressida, in Shakespeare's *Troilus and Cressida*, may —because of their sexual attractiveness—cause havoc in a man's world, but they are fickle rather than wicked, and their wantonness is a sympton of weakness, the frailty which is so often mentioned in relation to women, and which Sprenger saw as the reason for their vulnerability to the blandishments of the Devil. In a sense Helen and Cressida already represent body in opposition to mind, a distinction between masculine and feminine natures which was to be elaborated by later philosophers, and the noble men of the action were fools to wage war and be led astray by their appetites for such poor reasons. Helen and Cressida are both tarts by nature—neither of them are the type to see the error of their ways and return to a sense of fitness and honour by making an end of themselves. They swim with the tide. If degree is shaken to the core in *Troilus and Cressida* women are the cause, though Shakespeare does not blame the female sex, merely men for allowing themselves to be misled and beguiled.

If the moon is a female image it is because it also comes and goes, with the changeability and fickleness of women. Shakespeare's Cleopatra could easily have belonged to the tarts brigade, together with Helen and Cressida, but real passion gives her a new stature and dignity, and she does the right thing in killing herself:

My resolution's plac'd, and I have nothing
Of woman in me; now from head to foot
I am marble-constant, now the fleeting moon
No planet is of mine.

In part this passage takes its meaning from the belief that mutability was confined to the space beneath the moon, but irresolution is also equated with womanhood, and the whiteness of marble is compared with that of her body and the appearance, but not the reality, of the moon. And marble also speaks of death: corpses are supposed to look like marble, monuments to the dead are carved in it. Death is an honourable retreat for dishonoured women. In *A Winter's Tale* the process is reversed and an honourable wife whose name has been cleared appears as a statue who comes back to life: ' 'Tis time; descend; be stone no more.' But such reversals of the irreversible are confined to the magic of fairy tales. *Much Ado* has Hero presented to the repentant Claudio not as a statue, but as a cousin, since he is still of marriageable age.

Determination and strength of purpose were considered masculine qualities. The sun, which rises and sets each day as the same orb, is a masculine image. In patriarchal drama the women who go against their feminine nature, like Clytemnestra and Lady Macbeth, are aware of doing so. Even comic heroines who dress up as boys and swagger in male attire are liable to show their weakness when put to the test—as when Viola is challenged to a duel, for instance. Cleopatra's words show that she herself has internalized the concept of women as inconstant of purpose, weak by nature, and it was a commonplace of the period. Against *The Diall of Princes*, which may have been addressed mainly to persons of high rank, we can set the Elizabethan *Homilies*, which were intended for the instruction of the population at large:

> the woman is a weak creature, not endued with like strength and constancy of mind; therefore they be the sooner disquieted, and they be the more prone to all weak affections and dispositions of mind, more than men be; and lighter they be, and more vain in their phantasies and opinions.

Wives are enjoined in the *Homilies* to obey their husbands, and women are told that the acceptance of the griefs and perils of matrimony is their way of being good Christians. It is a perpetuation of the model of the patient Grizelda. In honouring her husband a woman honours God, and 'thou needest not to seek further for doing any better works'. Moreover, the *Homilies* go on, 'if thou canst suffer an extreme husband, thou shalt have great reward therefore'. A lot of contemporary drama was concerned with extreme husbands, though the rewards might seem to us to be minimal: in comedy a woman was rewarded by being taken back by a chastened and presumably somewhat less extreme husband, and in tragedy her rewards were in heaven, which was no doubt what the homilist had in mind.

In a patriarchal society a 'natural' woman is supposed to lack courage because men fear a courageous woman, for obvious reasons. She may rebel and turn against them. In Roscoe's book on the Baganda he writes: 'No disfigured or scarified woman could become the wife of a king; she was debarred on the ground that a woman who endured such pain was also capable of killing her husband.' He also writes that a pregnant woman who disliked her husband or had quarrelled with him might try to kill the child when she was delivered, a form of female revenge which reminds us of Medea and which may seem odd or barbaric to us, but which fits perfectly into the patriarchal system, where a woman was simply regarded as the bearer of the husband's child, but having no real part in its creation and no real claims on it. The patient Grizelda theme, so strong in the late Shakespearian romances, corroborates this patriarchal attitude to motherhood.

We have already seen what an important part the theme of revenge plays in both Athenian drama and the drama of Shakespeare's time. But women are not allowed to take revenge, because revenge implies not only courage, but rights. In a tribal situation it is the men who revenge their kinsmen, not women, who are regarded as property in this situation, and who are required to show grief, but not to take action. Under Athenian law, too, it was male kinsmen who took legal action in the case of violent death, while women merely changed guardianship. It behoved Electra to show grief at her father's death, but not to take revenge; she had to wait for her brother to do that, even though he might be dead or stay abroad for many years. Women who do take revenge, like Clytemnestra or Medea, take on a monstrous shape in the mind. In *The Insatiate Countess* it is a measure of Isabella's total depravity and monstrosity that she can declare

> *I'd not trust thunder with my fell revenge*
> *But mine own hands should do the dire exploit . . .*

When Gloucester's eyes are put out in *King Lear* the servants who witness this are shocked at what they have seen, but one is particularly shocked because a woman was involved:

> *If she live long,*
> *And, in the end, meet the old course of death,*
> *Women will all turn monsters.*

In his *Daemonologie* James I asserts that magicians are prompted mainly by curiosity (the old medieval sin of *curiositas* of which Faustus was guilty) but that witches are instigated mainly by the desire for revenge and worldly riches. Now revenge and worldly riches are two things which women cannot obtain by legitimate means in a patriarchal society. In addition, such fear of women as witches is based on guilt, the knowledge that women have good reason to be vengeful, since men regularly wrong and oppress them. For this reason the lid must be kept down: no woman must be allowed to take revenge, because in that case every woman would find cause. The fear of witchcraft as a revenge for wrongs done to women is also implicit in Sprenger's *Malleus Maleficarum*. Deserted sweethearts are apparently liable to bewitch their lovers, who become impotent with their lawful wives, whom God has joined. And the tradition of beggar woman as witch must also have its roots in guilt—charity denied becomes a curse.

The right to revenge is an inevitable part of the power structure in a tribal society, just as the right to take legal action to protect our persons and property is part of the power structure in a more developed society where the rights of enforcement have been taken away from the individual and placed in the power of a higher civic authority. Women can urge their menfolk to revenge, as Hieronimo's wife does in *The Spanish Tragedy*, or as Electra urges her brother Orestes, but they cannot take revenge themselves and remain within the accepted framework of ethics.

Nor do women appear as wielders of power in patriarchal drama. They are queens only by virtue of being wives. One can hardly count Cleopatra, who lives for love and is subject to the Romans in more senses than one. Shakespeare portrayed St Joan as a witch, which may be understandable in view of the fact that she led England's enemy to victory. But Boadicea, who might have been considered a very suitable subject for treatment in a period much concerned with nationalism and ancient British tradition, is conspicuously absent from the drama and literature of the period. Two plays survive on King Lear and his daughters, but there is no play about Cordelia as queen, though she would appear to provide good tragic material, since (according to Holinshed) she reigned for quite some time after her father's death and was eventually imprisoned by her nephews and killed herself. It is possible that the presence of a real queen on the throne of England was an inhibiting factor since political inferences could have been drawn from such a play. But it could equally be argued that a literary generation so bent on glorifying and mythologizing their queen might have been attracted to such a subject. But queens and empresses as rulers, whether indigenous or foreign, are conspicuously absent.

By the time of the Restoration women were playing female roles. By this time, too, the whole tone of drama had changed, and the old system of correspondences had broken down. People did not play a role within an organized system of values, they now played themselves. The social and metaphysical hierarchy had gone, and with it the old myth-making and quasi-ritual function of drama. It had become mere entertainment. Women were no longer portrayed in the essence of their womanhood by men, who would mimic and comment on female manners by their gestures and make-up; women now played themselves, attractive, worldly and relaxed in dramas of social exchange where people flirted and exchanged gossip and badinage. The actress as sex object appeared. Part of the aim of the performance was to display her charms, and men could compete for her favours. Actress, chorus girl, film starlet, the tradition has continued.

Middleton is the first dramatist whose plays show a clear change in the attitude to women. His plays contain critical comments on the social position of women, the fact that they are bought and sold in marriage, and his women are essentially like men, good or bad, like men, but no different in their motivations and desires. Significantly his witches are quite different from those in *Macbeth*. The witches in his play *The Witch* are not at all awe-inspiring—they handle a bag of tricks and the situation easily turns to comedy. Comparing the two Charles Lamb said, 'These Witches can hurt the body; those [ie. in *Macbeth*] have power over the soul.'

The seventeenth century was a period of increased opportunity for women, and on the whole they benefited from the social upheavals that followed the reign of James I. Their later oppression as wives and workers under the capitalist system is reflected in the novel rather than drama.

5 Order and Hierarchy

The more helpless man is in the face of a hostile environment, the greater his belief in sin as a cause of suffering, and the greater his need to expiate in ritual and sacrifice to avert further suffering. Human misfortune is hard to bear, but it becomes intolerable if no reason can be found for our suffering, and the reason must be found in human action, since this alone is open to human control. Thus the aborigine tribes studied by Spencer and Gillen did not accept the notion of natural death, but believed that 'a man who dies has of necessity been killed by some other man'; and Seligman, writing of the pagan tribes of the Nilotic Sudan, stated: 'The Azande believe that whatever the mode of death the real cause is witchcraft'.

Death may be caused by the evil intentions of another person, in which case vengeance is clearly called for. But it may also be caused by ones own wrongdoing. Evans-Pritchard, writing of the Nuer, reported that 'the most prominent feature of the worst forms of sin is that it kills', and Lienhardt made similar comments on the Dinka, who had the same word for a skin disease and for incest, since the disease was supposed to be its automatic sign and retribution. Such sin, the breaking of a social taboo, must be cleansed through ritual. Incest, for instance, was thought by the Dinka to result in barrenness unless ritual action was taken to overcome this. Obviously the original crime may not be known until its effects are felt, as happened in the case of Oedipus.

Within such a system of values it is not uncommon to have a legend placed in the dim and distant past which accounts for all suffering and death in the world. Thus the original sin of Adam and Eve brought suffering and death into the world; and the Dinka had their legend of the woman who disobeyed the divine commandment by using more than the daily grain of millet, thus bringing hunger, sickness and death to mankind.

It is within such a system of belief, a system of cause and effect which explains the suffering of the individual by linking it to the cosmos, that the tragic pattern can take shape. For this reason so much tragedy is concerned with the breaking of basic taboos —with incest, regicide, matricide and parricide. For this reason too the themes change somewhat as belief changes, and tragedy dies as the fundamental socio-religious beliefs lose their power and are replaced by scientific rationalism. Thunder ceases to be a divine portent and becomes mere electricity. Without taboos there can be no tragedy. It is for this reason that there is only one truly tragic subject in Western literature after the seventeenth century, and that is woman. She alone remains hedged in by taboos. Anna Karenina, Emma Bovary, Tess and Eustacia Vye have a tragic stature which no male fictional character of the period achieves, and their power and pathos derives from the fact that both for creator and reader they are battering their fragile frames against obstacles which appear immutable. By the end of the nineteenth century the dilemmas which man was heir to appeared man-made and therefore subject to social solutions. But woman's world remained fixed. Since men had created it they did not see the dilemmas of women as soluble through social reform. The taboos which surrounded woman were seen as inviolable, therefore she was still a potentially tragic figure in literature.

Although taboos may appear to have a religious base, their real base is social, just as the Ten Commandments are rules of social behaviour. In a society where law enforcement is weak social rules of behaviour come under divine sanction, particularly those rules of behaviour which are difficult to enforce, or where a breach is impossible to detect. 'Murder will out' is the cry in numerous Elizabethan and Greek dramas, and it usually comes out by supernatural means. Today we tend to put our faith not in ghosts, but in forensic laboratories and fingerprint experts.

Breaking a taboo means breaking a social law, and since drama is a social activity it tends to reinforce the social values of a particular society. An Athenian dramatist was not allowed to 'wrong the people', and there were plenty of safeguards to see that he did not offend the social values of the city, if he had any wish to do so. He was not only subject to censorship, but could not have proceeded with the performance of the play without the co-operation of the most wealthy and influential members of the community; finally he was subject to the approval of his audience by vote. Most dramatists are subject to such controls in varying degrees, whether the censorship is hidden or overt, comes from Church or State; and box office returns constitute another kind of censorship in the commercial theatre.

Because the breaking of taboos constitutes an offence against society there is one offence which overrides all others and which is implicit in all the other offences, and that is *hubris*. Incest is an offence against the property laws, since women come under the authority of men and are possessed by them. A young man commits hubris if he takes his father's wife, since his father has seniority. If he sleeps with his sister he is also offending his father, who has absolute authority to give his daughter away in marriage. These are the two most common forms of incest in tragic drama. As for murder, a tragic hero never comes to grief for murdering a servant or other social inferior, although he may become guilty of such an act in the course of the action. His initial murder or attempted murder, whether the killing is intended or accidental, is always perpetrated against a peer or social superior—father, nobleman or king. The latter for reasons already gone into, is the most heinous offence of all. If the main victim is the tragic protagonist's social inferior then that victim will usually be his own property, his wife or one of his children, and the tragedy arises from the fact that he has been led by circumstances to destroy his own dearest possessions.

Hubris can be against man or against God. If the protagonist is a king his offence is more likely to be against the latter, since he stands at the peak of the merely human pyramid. *Curiositas*, the sin of Faustus, was a form of hubris, since the limits of human knowledge had been fixed by God, and it was a sin to seek to know more. In so far as a woman was capable of hubris it was in rebellion against the male. Clytemnestra is guilty of that, and so is Medea.

A king had no difficulty in establishing his right to rule because of his divine descent, but perhaps man has always had more difficulty in maintaining his ascendancy over woman. Certainly there is a tendency to justify the subjection of woman by some form of original sin. The Christian Church justified its patriarchal attitudes on account of Eve's sin, a legend which is matched in many tribal societies, and the Greeks also had their legends which justified the total disenfranchisement of women. Aeschylus, who asserts the over-riding importance of patriarchy in the *Oresteia*, justifies the position of women to the Athenian audience by recalling the story of the massacre of Lemnos, when jealous wives on the island conspired to murder their husbands, and all male Lemnians, together with their concubines:

> *Yes, of all crimes remembered, one stands first:*
> *The Lemnian massacre, a tale*
> *To make men groan with heartsickness.*
> *And when they speak, all pale,*
> *Of some new outrage, 'It is as bad,' they say,*
> *'As what occurred in Lemnos.' So to this day,*
> *By gods detested, our whole sex is cursed,*
> *By men disfranchised, scorned, and portionless;*
> *For no man honours what the gods abhor.*

The hate comes primarily from God, and is merely endorsed and obeyed by men. And the fact that the words are spoken by the female chorus only helps to internalize the message for the audience, since the 'women' in the chorus obviously do not dispute the judgment on their sex.

So the tragic pattern derives from the belief that suffering must be the result of some transgression against immutable laws, although the original transgression may not have been intentional. In fact the divine laws are social and human, integral to the fabric of human society.

Once such a sin against divine law has been discovered on account of its consequences, these have to be averted or reversed through ritual purification. The Aristotelian concept of catharsis in relation to tragedy really only makes sense when we understand that Greek tragedy functioned in a society still dominated by such beliefs. Thus tragedy could be justified as a form of purification at second hand, so to speak. 'Our pity,' wrote Aristotle, 'is excited by misfortunes undeservedly suffered, and our terror by some resemblance between the sufferer and ourselves.' If misfortunes are undeservedly suffered it is because, within this system of belief, intention does not affect the consequence of one's action; ie. if you kill a person by accident you may be just as polluted as in the case of a premeditated murder. The audience are reminded that the punishment can be out of all proportion to the apparent heinousness of the offence, and the resemblance between the protagonist and the audience ensures that the audience will be cleansed even before it has committed an offence by the awful warning which the play provides. Thus tragedy fulfils a useful social purpose, since the *miasma* or pollution of the individual affects the entire community. The identification between audience and tragic protagonist is reinforced by Aristotle's definition of the ideal tragic hero as someone who is neither very wicked nor particularly virtuous; ie. someone very like you and me. His character should be 'that of a person neither eminently virtuous or just, nor yet involved in misfortune by deliberate vice or villainy, but by some error of human frailty'. But he probably misunderstood the real reason for tragic protagonists being of royal blood, since he regarded tragedy as having its beginning in 'little myths and ridiculous diction'. Obviously it seems appropriate that tragedy should come to 'someone of high fame and flourishing prosperity', since he that is low need fear no fall, but he seems to have missed the true significance of kingship which these apparently stupid myths embodied, presumably because the beliefs were too remote from his own era and political inclinations.

The one thing that unites all critics and commentators throughout the ages is the belief that wickedness must not be shown to flourish unpunished. Plato was not concerned with aesthetics, but with the influence of poets on society. In the *Laws* he insisted that poets should always show good men as leading good lives and bad men as coming to a bad end: 'I should impose all but the heaviest of penalties on anyone in the land who should declare that any wicked men lead pleasant lives, or that things profitable and lucrative are different from things just.' (*Book II*)

But if a dramatist is to achieve a cosy equation between virtue and happiness he has to work within an understood ethical framework. Greek tragedy was far from cosy because, within the framework of a belief in taboo and pollution, the punishment could be out of all proportion to the offence. However, many writers regard the punishment of crime as a social expediency rather than a cosmic necessity. Corneille, for instance, who claimed to have revived and even improved on the classical tragic tradition, maintained that the rewarding of good actions and the punishment of the wicked was not an artistic precept but a social custom necessitated by audience expectation. He regarded this moral expectation as a modern refinement unknown to the barbaric Greeks with their curious religious superstitions.

Drama, whether broadcast by modern television or part of tribal ritual, has a central function in enforcing and perpetuating the ideology of a society (and as well as perpetuating, it of course also becomes a vital element in the dialectic of social change). The Athenians realized this and used dramatic festivals to create a sense of political identity within the *polis*. They even saw this sense of identity as necessary for its survival, and the poet's function as crucial. To ensure that the entire population attended these dramatic festivals, the poor were subsidized to enable them to attend, and the entire organization was at once a civic responsibility and an honour for the wealthier citizens who sponsored the event.

Later societies have also recognized the quite peculiar power of drama as a social and moral influence. Censorship is one form of that recognition, the closing of theatres by religious or political factions is another. Schlegel linked the orator and the dramatist in their power to break through conventional reserves, and the Athenians, like other societies before and since, in effect made little distinction between the theatre of entertainment and that of the political assembly, or, for that matter,the courts of justice. Great stress was laid on a politician's ability to move the populace by his powers of oratory. Later political assemblies were actually held in the theatre. Justice also had its theatrical aspect. According to Glotz,

> Defendants surrounded themselves on the tribune with their kinsmen, their wife and weeping children in order to soften the hearts of the judges. On all sides play was made with patriotism or devotion to democracy. As soon as a case touched upon politics the tribunal was transformed into a public assembly.[1]

It is not difficult to think of modern parallels, whether in courtroom drama or the drama of Parliament. And both involve playing to the gallery.

If drama demands a kind of group consensus which is not so necessary for other forms of artistic expression, the fact that the theatre involves a crowd is also very important. Everyone knows that crowd behaviour is very different from the behaviour of individuals. A novel or poem read in the privacy of the home will have a very different effect from a play watched as part of a group. Schlegel recognized this element in drama:

> Almost inconceivable is the power of a visible communion of numbers to give intensity to those feelings of the heart which usually retire into privacy . . . The faith in the validity of such emotions becomes irrefragable from its diffusion; we feel ourselves strong among so many associates, and all hearts and minds flow together in one great and irresistible stream. On this very account the privilege of influencing an assembled crowd is exposed to most dangerous abuses.[2]

Drama certainly derives some of its potency from the fact that we are part of a large audience, from the feeling that we in some sense participate in the action, from the rhythm of verse and music and dance which influences our senses. Spencer and Gillen were not slow to notice the influence exerted on individual tribesmen once they became involved in group activity. They also described wild, orgiastic corroborees. But there is no doubt that the dramatic performances we have described earlier were embarked on with great solemnity and were controlled by tradition. It is doubtful whether a theatrical audience is really open to the degree of dangerous abuse that Schlegel feared, since a theatrical performance cannot come into existence at all without a certain social consensus to start with, after which the audience sits in judgment on the play, either by box office returns, or by the Athenian system of voting, or by booing or applause. Drama functions within a system of socially accepted values, so that a dramatist can only function successfully if he conforms to the accepted beliefs and values of his time and place. He may be allowed to challenge some of the values, particularly if a section of the society in which he lives is already beginning to question them, but he is unlikely to succeed in presenting a total challenge to existing beliefs. So an evil dramatist could only flourish in an evil society.

All drama therefore functions within a moral framework, corresponding to the moral values of the society within which it is produced. Ibsen's plays may have been thought shocking by many of his contemporaries, but he was in fact expressing beliefs which were already widely current, about the hypocrisy of bourgeois society, for example, and the social imprisonment of women. Similarly the plays of Euripides must have reflected a changed attitude to religion and the individual in relation to society, even though conservatives might have thought him decadent and lacking in the old moral fibre of Aeschylus. In our own day dramatic output is much more fragmented; we do not have one theatre but many, and no only theatres but cinemas and television sets. It is significant that moral codes are most strictly observed in mass entertainment which, in the second half of the twentieth century, is television. Theatres, largely patronized by a sophisticated élite, challenge many of the traditional values—sexual, political and social. But these are rarely, if ever, challenged on television. Instead the masses are fed on an unchanging diet of police stories which glorify the precepts of law and order and the rights of property. Crime is always dealt with efficiently, murder will always out. The same values are reiterated in westerns, which allows industrial man to indulge a fantasy view of himself into the bargain. Sexual permissiveness reaches the small screen last of all, and then only in a very modified form.

But although all drama functions within a moral framework this does not necessarily make it tragic. Tragedy depends, not on crime and punishment, but on a justification of the sum total of human suffering through some form of inner necessity, and this necessity in turn implies some sort of order that runs through all things, cosmic laws of cause and effect that determine human destiny and which man must attempt to understand in order to avoid disaster. It is by breaking such cosmic laws, not merely human ones, that man meets a tragic fate. Implicit in this cosmic view is the notional hope that, could one only have a full understanding of these laws and comply with them, misfortune could be avoided. In Greek tragedies this notional hope is expressed by the choruses or some humble character, and there is a strong suggestion that sticking to one's own humble station in life, knowing one's place, and conformity may protect one from tragedy.

Although the laws are regarded as cosmic or divine, they are in fact human laws, and have to do with the way society orders itself, or the way society believes itself to function, which may not necessarily be the same thing. Most of us probably feel that comedy often provides us with a more realistic and recognizable portrayal of human behaviour than tragedy, because in tragedy a man is never merely a man but part of a whole cosmic structure, indivisible from his role in that structure, and the structure tends to be idealized. In order to show that a man will be punished for breaking cosmic laws it is also necessary to show the 'right' way to behave, and this may bear very little relationship to life as it is actually lived. If tragedy shows us a world where women should be (and therefore presumably are for the most part) obedient, silent and chaste, a world where it is mete for the young to respect the old, and for kings to be both kingly and semi-divine, this is likely to be a portrayal of the world which strains our credulity unless tension is raised and upheld by high-flown language and poetic imagery. It may also be upheld by rhythm, and—in the case of Greek drama and Japanese Noh theatre—by music, dance, and a high degree of stylization in form and gesture which gives the audience the impression, not of reality, but a higher reality of some sort. No wonder that in both cases the tension needed to be broken by a worldly rough and tumble, some light relief where ordinary people were seen behaving in the way ordinary people are apt to do, a world where women can nag and their husbands can want to get away from them, a world where old men can be tiresome and foolish rather than sage.

This is not to say that tragedy functions within a framework of a totally idealized view of the world, but in order to believe in a fall from grace it is necessary to believe in grace; breaking laws implies the existence of law, disorder implies a falling away from order. The idea of a cosmic order also implies, if not a totally static view of the world and human society, at least a continuum. The Christian religion, for instance, has in past times provided a continuous view of history, one which could explain misfortune, disruption and change in terms of original sin, and we have already seen how, during Shakespeare's day, history was seen in moral terms, a curious amalgam of fact with Biblical and classical mythology. This is not to say that the days of such a view of history are necessarily over. It seems to me that the Marxist interpretation of history is in many ways similar—closed, cosmic and moral. A society which had sufficiently internalized such a view of the world could presumably produce effective tragic heroes, protagonists who did not merely behave in an antisocial way, or go against the will of the majority, but who actually set their faces against the immutable forces of history and the cosmic order, and thus brought about their own downfall. The difference between tragedy and propaganda is in the degree of internalization of the values and concepts. Not until this internalization has taken place can a dramatist create a character who is not merely a fool or villain, but someone who can evoke our sympathy, and with whom we can identify.

A cosmic view of the world, with laws which cannot be infringed without inevitable suffering and punishment not only provides a satisfactory explanation for human misery, it is also an important factor in consensus politics. Every society needs a certain degree of consensus, but in some areas there is more need for an explanatory mythology, which drama provides. Hereditary privilege involving, as it does, gross inequalities, needs a religious mythology to support it; so does the authority of kings, and the subjection of women to men. We have already seen that the Greeks tended to put under divine sanction those laws which they were least able to enforce by human means. It could be argued that the reason why our television screens give us endless stories of police detectives solving crimes is because in reality a very tiny proportion of crimes ever do get solved. And it is important to remember that during Shakespeare's day nobody even believed, as they do now, in the possibility of law enforcement. Murder in high places was a commonplace, and no doubt lesser folk also got away with it with alarming frequency. People resorted to ritual magic to find out who was responsible for a theft. Once we get to simple tribal societies, like those studied by Spencer and Gillen, there is a total dependence on group consensus, and therefore group mythology and its ritual enactment take on a particular importance. In addition drama festivals become occasions when people come together in large groups to take part in group activities. The drama itself may emphasize structure—social, political or religious—but the occasion emphasizes communitas.

If tragedy provides a paradigm of structure, comedy not only provides much needed relief from the high tension of tragedy, it also gives an image of anti-structure, of status-reversal as opposed to hierarchy, but one which is always temporary. Servants may play master, wives may play tricks on their husbands, but finally order is restored: misunderstandings end in marriages, harmony is restored, the servant goes back to his quarters and the master doffs his humble disguise. The status-reversal we find in comedy has its parallels in social rituals, particularly in those societies which have a rigid social structure. The custom of having a Lord of Misrule during Christmas celebrations in great households and turning the hierarchy upside down depended on an implicit recognition of the true hierarchy for all the other weeks of the year. It might be a great joke to have a man of no rank as master of ceremonies, but *Mis*rule implies its opposite, which is proper rule. And even such temporary licence can be taken too far—we see what happens to Malvolio when he steps out of line and seriously considers himself worthy of his mistress's hand in marriage. The servants and hangers-on are the first to jeer at such presumption. In *Twelfth Night* merry-making is combined with a distinct recognition of one's own place in the world. Malvolio's misguided presumption is an aspect of his Puritanism.

For the aborigines, for the Greeks, for the Elizabethans, social order was equated with natural order to a very large extent, and this enabled a dramatist to work within a cosmic framework and make references which for a modern man seem merely 'poetic' but which a contemporary audience would have understood and accepted without any such qualification. The way in which the social and political chaos in *King Lear* is mirrored in the chaos of the elements during the storm is perhaps the most obvious example. Later such an equivalence became a mere poetic device, and critics labelled it the 'pathetic fallacy', but there was nothing fallacious about it for Shakespeare's contemporaries, who were used to seeing auguries for political events in the heavens, just as their forefathers had done since the beginning of time. Before discussion began in the Athenian assembly a religious ceremony including animal sacrifice was performed, and the session was suspended in case of storm, earthquake or eclipse, since these were regarded as a sign from Zeus.

One such equation between natural and social order is a respect for seniority. Spencer and Gillen quoted the example of a medicine man who lost his powers after trying to strike one of the older men, a good example of the total internalization of social laws.

When political functions are distributed amongst the male

population according to age, the most significant distinction is often between men of fighting age and those who are too old to fight, and who become concerned with ritual, the discussion of public affairs and the settling of disputes. This ties in well with the equation of age and wisdom, particularly in a society where traditional rites and mythologies are handed down by word of mouth, as was the case amongst aborigine tribes, where the elders held the secrets of the churinga stores, passed on the myths and rituals, and were given special marks of respect by younger men. Such marks of respect often include the duty to give food to elders. In this way a generation which has become too old to fend for itself is kept alive.

Seniority was very much a feature of political life in the Greek city state. At Sparta one could not enter the Apella before the age of thirty, and one could not become a *geron* until the age of sixty. In the early days of the Athenian assembly the herald opened the debate with the words 'Who amongst the Athenians over fifty wishes to speak?' after which the question was put progressively to the younger men. Later this system was modified, but younger men were still not allowed to speak first.

This respect for old age is endorsed by Plato in the *Laws*, where he makes it clear that both a system of seniority among men and a belief in the gods is necessary to maintain a stable society:

> the older is greatly more revered than the younger, both among the gods and among those men who propose to keep safe and happy. An outrage perpetrated by a younger against an older person is a shameful thing to see happening in a State, and a thing hateful to God; when a young man is beaten by an older man, it is meet that, in every case, he should quietly endure his anger, and thus quietly store up honour for the time of his own old age. (*Book IX*)

> . . . none of the youth shall inquire which laws are wrong and which right, but all shall declare in unison, with one mouth and one voice, that all are rightly established by divine enactment, and shall turn a deaf ear to anyone who

> says otherwise; and further, that if any old man has any stricture to pass on any of your laws, he must not utter such views in the presence of any young man, but before a magistrate or one of his own age. (*Book I*)

In spite of the sophisticated political machinery developed in the Athenian city state the Athenians continued to regard law as sacred. From religious scruple the Assembly did not take upon itself the right to abolish existing laws and make new ones; instead it legislated by decree. Since the law was sacred the author of a decree which interfered with existing law had to avert malediction and penalty by coming as a suppliant to beg for pardon, and the immunity he sought could only be accorded to him in a plenary assembly, by a vote of at least six thousand, taken by secret ballot. Such customs did not outgrow their origins because it was felt that bad laws were better than laws which were constantly being changed.

Plato emphasizes the need for all citizens, but particularly the younger generation, to have an unquestioning belief in the divine enactment of the city's laws. By the end of his life he seems to have returned to a traditional conservatism, and in the *Laws* he maintains that religion must be invoked for the sake of social stability:

> it is of the highest importance that our arguments, showing that the gods exist and that they are good and honour justice more than do men, should by all means possess some degree of persuasiveness; for such a prelude is the best we could have in defence, as one may say, of all our laws. (*Book X*)

Respect for seniority is implicit in those Greek plays which have survived and great wisdom—that of the seer, for instance—is equated with advanced years. It is only in the status reversal of comedy, in Aristophanes for example, that old men can be shown as foolish.

During Shakespeare's lifetime old age was still equated with wisdom and experience rather than with failing powers. Ralegh, in *The Cabinet-Council*, wrote that advisers to a prince should be older men: 'The election of counsellors is and ought to be chiefly among men of long experience and grave years.' In a relatively early play, *Richard II*, this equation of seniority with wisdom is still adhered to. John of Gaunt expresses a collective nationalism with his dying, if prolific breath and gives his young sovereign advice which the latter sneers at. By the time Shakespeare wrote *King Lear* he had, however, come to understand a deeper tragic irony, that old men do not necessarily become wise. Nevertheless Goneril and Regan are wrong to treat their father with disrespect, as someone in his dotage, just as Lear had been wrong to upset the hierarchy of seniority by abdicating in favour of his children. *Gorboduc*, lacking such inspired vision, emphasizes in a much more simplistic and less cynical fashion, that natural, political and social order all require that the old should not abrogate their responsibility to rule over the young.

Lear is not only a king, he is also a father, and the right of a parent to command the respect of his children was long regarded as the most fundamental 'natural' law. It is another of those basic tenets on which the fabric of a society depends when there is no complex infrastructure. In the Old Testament 'Honour your father and your mother' is the first of the ten commandments concerned with relations between human beings, as opposed to observances due to God: it comes even before the commandment not to commit murder. Plato endorses the right of parents to rule over their children, which was why he regarded parricide and matricide as deserving of 'a hundred deaths', a view which is certainly reflected in the Greek drama which has survived. Plato gives a rather glib summing up of the social order as both just and biological in the *Laws*, and it is a justification of hierarchy which the Elizabethans would have understood and endorsed:

> Now the better are the superior of the worse, and the older in general of the younger; wherefore also parents are superior to their offspring, men to women and children, rulers to ruled. (*Book XI*)

Like all authority which cannot easily be enforced, the law which requires children to respect their parents is one particularly emphasized by divinity. The parental curse is therefore considered to have particular potency. Evans-Pritchard has this to say in *Nuer Religion*:

> The curse of father or mother is serious. A man may curse his son for constant disobedience and for meanness, especially for refusing him meat. Indeed, any old man may curse a youth for refusing him food . . . A mother may curse her son for neglect, especially when she is old and must rely on others for support . . . a person standing in any social relationship to another may curse him if he has been wronged by him. However, the more distant the relationship the less effective the curse, because the less obligation and therefore the less wrong. (*pp. 165–6*)

In Greek drama parents threaten their children with the parental curse—Clytemnestra asks Orestes, for instance, whether he does not fear her curse. As long as faith in a natural social order under divine protection held good the parental curse was still an effective weapon. Lear's curse on Cordelia must have sounded portentous to a contemporary audience, and prepared them for her tragic end—it is significant that later audiences who no longer believed in the old divine sanctions found her death too shocking and actually changed the ending. If Cordelia is allowed to live the old pattern of beliefs is nullified.

However, the old pattern of beliefs is continually questioned in *King Lear*, even if finally endorsed. The Fool acts as commentator, stands outside the conflict (rather like a chorus) and tells us what the action exemplifies: that the world is corrupt, that survival depends on keeping your wits about you, and that it is dangerous to grow old *without* growing wise. It is part of the irony and conflict inherent in the play that Lear, who so often invokes divine sanction to so little effect, should in this instance utter a curse which does take effect and, like a boomerang, returns to break his own heart. We tend to ignore the fact that Goneril and Regan have also become subject to a father's curse

(Goneril has in fact been cursed at some length) because we take it for granted that they should be exterminated. Their survival would indeed have outraged not only contemporary sensibilities, but our own. We may have lost respect for old age but we still demand that murder and wanton cruelty should not be seen to go unpunished.

Order implies hierarchy. Apparent injustice can be transformed into natural justice by making human hierarchy part of a cosmic order. Thus what is 'natural' and what is 'moral' become fused. In Shakespeare's period they spoke of degree, and the degrees of men had a system of correspondences in the animal, vegetable and mineral world. Tillyard, in *The Elizabethan World Picture*, quotes Sir John Fortescue, the fifteenth-century jurist:

> God created as many different kinds of things as he did creatures, so that there is no creature which does not differ in some respect from all other creatures and by which it is in some respect superior or inferior to all the rest. So that from the highest angel down to the lowest of his kind there is absolutely not found an angel that has not a superior and inferior; nor from man down to the meanest worm is there any creature which is not in some respect superior or inferior to another.

Thus the whole of nature is involved in a complex network, not only of interdependence, but of rank and value. It is right that kings should rule over commoners; it is right that the bird should swallow the worm. We see that the hierarchy includes God and the angels, just as the differences between gods and men were, for the Greeks, essentially differences of rank, particularly in Homer, where they seem overlords in the feudal system.

Thus hubris becomes the cardinal sin of tragedy, the offence embodied in all other offences. Children must not step out of line and rebel against their parents, women must not turn against their husbands, or commoners against their king. Most important of all, kings must not overreach their own limitations and call down the wrath of their superiors, the gods, since divine wrath is the most potent of all. The tragic consequences of hubris are embodied in the Christian religion: one angel was guilty of it and thus brought conflict into the cosmos in the person of Satan.

It could be argued that Shakespeare, like Plato, finally endorsed a conservative view of the world because the alternatives seemed too terrible to contemplate. He came very close to seeing a terrible, anarchic universe in *King Lear* and seems to have opted for the rather trite pieties of Edgar and Albany to round off the play as a drowning man will clutch at a straw. The idea that 'the gods are just' has been belied by the action. Elsewhere, notably in *Troilus and Cressida*, he gives a more reasoned argument for subscribing to the traditional view of degree, and it is rather like the reasoning behind Plato's *Laws*—anarchy must be avoided at all costs. One immediate consequence which Ulysses names as a result of taking degree away is that 'the rude son should strike his father dead'. The ultimate consequence would be that man would become prey to his own uncontrolled appetite. This is a possibility also mentioned in *King Lear*—by Albany. Without divine intervention and punishment, he says,

> *Humanity must perforce prey on itself,*
> *Like monsters of the deep.*

And we are given a significant example of what can happen when degree is taken away. After a servant has witnessed the blinding of Gloucester he says of Cornwall:

> *I'll never care what wickedness I do*
> *If this man comes to good.*

Take but degree away, and you not only have sons rebelling against their fathers, but servants against their masters. Behind the concept of lords and princes setting a moral example to their inferiors is the need to maintain the myth of social superiors being moral superiors, in order to maintain the hierarchy at all.

It was because Machiavelli challenged this view that he was so deeply hated and distrusted in England; that as late as 1640 Edward Dacres, in the introduction to the first translation of *The Prince*, could write that 'his Maximes and Tenents are condemnd of all, as pernicious to all Christian States, and hurtfull to all human Societies'. But, he adds, 'if thou consider well the actions of the world, thou shalt find him much practised by those that condemn him'. Ulysses's long speech on the necessity of degree seems out of all proportion to the requirements of the action in *Troilus and Cressida*, nor do the other characters in the play have any opposing views to put forward to warrant such a long speech; Ulysses—ie. Shakespeare—is arguing with someone who is not in the play at all, and that person is Machiavelli. Having described the awfulness of a universe without degree, one that Shakespeare was soon to come close to realizing in *King Lear*, the speech goes on to list elements in human society which depend on degree, and it reads like a summary of many of Shakespeare's own plays: 'brotherhood in cities' reminds us of *Romeo and Juliet*, written in the same year as the English translation of Machiavelli's own *Florentine History* appeared, with its descriptions of the stresses placed on the city by feuding families and their supporters; whilst 'primogenitive and due of birth' together with 'Prerogative of age, crowns, sceptres' reminds us of half a dozen earlier plays in which these concepts provided the moral fabric of the entire structure, as well as looking forward to *King Lear* where that fabric came close to being torn to shreds. If we need conclusive evidence that Ulysses/Shakespeare is in fact giving us a long argument against the political ideas of Machiavelli we have, I think, conclusive proof in the lines

> *Degree being vizarded*
> *The unworthiest shows as fairly in the mask.*

Now the art of dissimulation was the aspect of Machiavellian thought which was most familiar to Shakespeare's contemporaries, particularly in the theatre, where the idea had found its expression in the stock character of the machiavell, the villain who schemes and plots to his own advantage whilst appearing to be an honest man. Edmund, of course, belongs to this category. The speech then goes on to say that the heavens observe degree, but that

> *when the planets*
> *In evil mixture to disorder wander,*
> *What plagues, and what portents, what mutiny,*
> *What raging of the sea, shaking of earth,*
> *Commotion in the winds, frights, changes, horrors,*
> *Divert and crack, rend and deracinate*
> *The unity and married calm of states*
> *Quite from their fixure!*

These are precisely the views of Gloucester which Edmund mocks in his father. The trouble is that Edmund, and not his rather foolish father, has intelligence and modernity on his side. Machiavelli also had intelligence and modernity on his side, which was probably why Shakespeare, using Ulysses as a mouthpiece, found it necessary to argue against him at such length.

The world view to which Shakespeare clung had not much longer to run. Perhaps his own doubts on the feasibility of a natural order that was at once a moral and social one led him to turn to an ideal world of romance, to the magic of Prospero, who could control the warring elements and the raging sea for the benefit of humanity. But if the old framework was no longer feasible, tragedy itself would no longer be feasible. The tragic hero moved within a cosmic framework where, since order was divinely ordained, rebellion against it was a cardinal sin. His action was like a stone dropped into still water, producing concentric rings in ever-widening circles. But while the framework still held, it was unusually rich in metaphor because of the system of correspondences, whereby the pattern of human events was mirrored in the stars and paralleled in the animal and vegetable kingdom.

That the system of correspondences, the wealth of metaphor

attached to the image of a divinely ordered universe, was accessible and familiar to the general public even if they did not go to the theatre we know, for instance, from the Elizabethan *Homilies*, written to be read in churches throughout the land, and thus familiar to more than an educated and literate élite. The homily on—significantly—obedience, begins with an exposition of the concept of degree, a universal order which keeps all things and all human beings in a state of balance, but which also requires a state of obedience from all those within the hierarchy, wife to husband, child to parent, subject to ruler, and ruler to God:

> Almighty God hath created and appointed all things in heaven, earth, and waters, in a most excellent and perfect order. In heaven he hath appointed distinct and several orders and states of archangels and angels. In earth he hath assigned and appointed kings, princes, with other governors under them, in all good and necessary order. The water above is kept, and raineth down in due time and season. The sun, moon, stars, rainbow, thunder, lightning, clouds, and all birds of the air, do keep their order. The earth, trees, seeds, plants, herbs, corn, grass, and all manner of beasts, keep themselves in their order. All the parts of the whole year, as winter, summer, months, nights and days, continue in their order. All kinds of fishes in the sea, rivers, and waters; with all fountains, springs; yea, the seas themselves, keep their comely course and order. And man himself also hath all his parts within and without; as soul, heart, mind, memory, understanding, reason, speech, with all and singular corporal members of his body, in a profitable, necessary, and pleasant order. Every degree of people in their vocation, calling, and office, hath appointed to them their duty and order: some are in high degree, some in low; some kings and princes, some inferiors and subjects; priests and laymen, masters and servants, fathers and children, husbands and wives, rich and poor; and every one have need of other: so that in all things is to be lauded and praised the goodly order of God; without the which no house, no city, no commonwealth, can continue and endure, or last. For

> where there is no right order, there reigneth all abuse, carnal liberty, enormity, sin, and Babylonical confusion. Take away kings, princes, rulers, magistrates, judges, and such estates of God's order; no man shall ride or go by the highway unrobbed; no man shall sleep in his own house or bed unkilled; no man shall keep his wife, children, and possessions in quietness; all things shall be common: and there must needs follow all mischief and utter destruction of souls, bodies, goods, and commonwealths.

A homily on the iniquities of rebellion is particularly thunderous. The public are reminded that all the miseries of the world stemmed from the rebellion of Lucifer, that monarchs are ordained by God, and that the Almighty never fails to punish the rebel in the end. Rebellion is not merely a crime against the state, but against the whole of humanity. And the idea of the body politic as a kind of biological body, so familiar in Shakespeare, is also propagated in the homily on rebellion; a subject must not presume to judge his superior: 'what a perilous thing were it to commit unto the subjects the judgment, which prince is wise and godly . . . as though the foot must judge of the head'. The implication being, of course, that intelligence and reason reside in the head, which gives rulers the right to rule. It was a commonplace image during Elizabeth's reign, but even as late as 1640 we find the first translator of Machiavelli's *The Prince* arguing against many of Machiavelli's views on rulers on the basis that the head 'is but a member of the body', the implication being that the state is an organic whole and a ruler would not do anything contrary to the true interests of his subjects. Eight years later the concept was doomed for good when the body chopped off the royal head and managed to keep marching on without the assistance of royal brains.

The concept of social order within which tragedy can function implies a divine hierarchy: human beings must be careful not to overstep the limitations of their own social position. The kind of sentiments expressed in the *Homilies* (using the Church as a mouthpiece for the State) are reflected in some of the inscriptions found on Apollo's temple at Delphi:

Curb thy spirit.
Observe the limit.
Hate hubris.
Keep a reverent tongue.
Fear authority.
Bow before the divine.
Glory not in strength.
Keep woman under rule.

In tragedy it is often humble people, the chorus or a servant who, seeing their social superiors come to grief, express thankfulness for their own humble position in life. The audience, identifying with these characters, are thus encouraged to think themselves lucky rather than deprived or oppressed. Take the nurse in the *Medea* of Euripides for instance:

To have learnt to live on the common level
Is better. No grand life for me,
Just peace and quiet as I grow old.
The middle way, neither great nor mean,
Is best by far, in name and practice.
To be rich and powerful brings no blessing;
Only more utterly
Is the prosperous house destroyed, when the gods are angry.

In Elizabethan and Jacobean tragedy we are often told that a head which wears a crown does not sleep easily, and the burdens of authority are emphasized. We hear very little about the burdens of poverty—except in *King Lear*, where Lear finds himself face to face with the realities of beggary. Perhaps another sign of the fabric beginning to crack. 'I have ta'en/Too little care of this' he says, and condemns not only himself but, by implication, all monarchs, and the system itself. In the last act we have one of Edgar's conventional pieties: 'The Gods are just', but Lear implies that until rulers create a more egalitarian society there is no justice in heaven:

Take physic, Pomp;
Expose thyself to feel what wretches feel,
That thou mayst shake the superflux to them,
And show the Heavens more just.

This goes right against the concept of a divine order where the rich man should stay in his castle and the poor man at his gate. Shakespeare seems to have shied away from the implications of his own vision, as he shied away from the implications of a Machiavellian view of politics. Who knows how far he avoided the expression of political unorthodoxy and a dangerous radicalism in order to hold onto his own position and, possibly, his head?

Within this framework of a cosmic and human hierarchy hubris is inevitably the sin endemic in all other sins, and patience the greatest virtue. In his suffering Lear calls for patience, a quality which he has never needed before, when he was a powerful ruling monarch. Patience is a virtue which belongs to the underdog. Subjects were exhorted to suffer the wrongdoings of a bad monarch patiently in sixteenth-century England, whilst the patient wife had long been a stock type in patriarchal societies: Andromache, Penelope, St Augustine's mother, Grizelda. And just as men must accept the arbitrary rule of their overlords, and women the arbitrary rule of their husbands, all human beings must accept the arbitrary dictates of higher powers. Just as Grizelda is tested, so Job is tested. At first he insisted on being given a reason—'Let the Almighty state his case against me!'—but it is only later that he realizes that the Almighty has no need to do any such thing, and that he must suffer unquestioningly. Significantly, Job was first tested as a result of a challenge from Satan, the patron saint of hubris.

It was largely through Seneca that Elizabethan dramatists inherited the non-Christian tradition of hubris. Seneca is very explicit on the heaviness of crowns on human heads and the fact that a humble station in life is something to be thankful for. 'What king is happy on his throne?' exclaims his Oedipus. 'Truly the hand of Fate/Is kinder to the humble' say the chorus in his *Phaedra*. He was extolled by his sixteenth-century English defenders for his unparalleled morality amongst heathen writers, and his mode of bewailing the burdens of high office was in some cases directly imitated.

If hubris is implicit in the offences of all tragic protagonists, the most overtly hubristic heroes are those of Marlowe. His Faustus is guilty of hubris in trying to go beyond the bounds of human knowledge set down by God, whilst Tamburlaine, unlike Agamemnon in the *Oresteia*, ignores the boundaries set by God on the activities and powers of human monarchs. Both these characters seem to be asking for a sticky end. 'A sound magician is a mighty god,' exclaims Faustus, which would lead any spectator to see trouble in store. 'A god,' declares Tamburlaine, 'is not as glorious as a king'. Faustus is foolish enough to ignore a warning from Mephestophilis himself:

> Faustus: *Was not that Lucifer an angel once?*
> Meph: *Yes, Faustus, and most dearly lov'd of God.*
> Faustus: *How comes it, then, that he is prince of devils?*
> Meph: *O, by aspiring pride and insolence;*
> *For which God threw him from the face of heaven.*

You would think a man of learning would have taken the hint, but both Tamburlaine and Faustus seem drunk with their own potential. Jove, declares Tamburlaine, must be afraid of being overthrown, and he finally sees himself making war on the heavens. 'Come, let us march against the powers of heaven' he declares when sickness strikes him down. His pretensions, like those of Faustus, seem ludicrous, but Marlowe's capacity to take off on imaginative flights of poetry give such human errors an unexpected grandeur. Marlowe may seem to get intoxicated with his themes, but there is still a moral for the audience to swallow:

> *Faustus is gone: regard his hellish fall,*
> *Whose fiendful fortune may exhort the wise,*
> *Only to wonder at unlawful things,*
> *Whose deepness doth entice such forward wits*
> *To practise more than heavenly power permits.*

But the world where men could not experiment with hidden knowledge was fast disappearing. Science would take over from magic. Likewise, the world of pre-ordained authorities was also to vanish in the near future. With the bourgeois revolution of Cromwell and the death of Charles I, the concept of a divinely ordered social hierarchy disappeared for good. The Church as a bastion of that authority also vanished, to be replaced by the Puritan conscience where each man was answerable to himself. For the poet trying to work within the old tradition this created a dilemma, exemplified by Milton, who tried to work within the tragic tradition, which he admired, but could not resolve the dilemmas created by hubris, rebellion and original sin on the one hand, and the concept of free will and the individual conscience on the other. Before, it had been possible to explain inordinate human suffering in terms of a divine pattern, because the breaking of taboos did not need to be conscious in order to bring down punishment. But a religion which emphasized free will, the individual conscience, and tended to ascribe to God the same rational enlightenment which it valued in human kind, could not possibly make the old tragic tradition work and find an explanation for arbitrary disasters and undeserved suffering, even if it had been possible to find someone to play the part of the deposed king. Donne got nearer to the truth when, in 'The First Anniversary', he complained that 'new Philosophy calls all in doubt':

> *'Tis all in peeces, all cohaerence gone;*
> *All just supply, and all Relation:*
> *Prince, Subject, Father, Sonne, are things forgot,*
> *For every man alone thinkes he hath got*
> *To be a Phoenix, and that then can bee*
> *None of that kinde, of which he is, but hee.*

A passage prophetic of the whole romantic movement in literature, with its isolated individualism and Prometheus unbound as an impossible hero. The common humanity of the social contract which ultimately replaced the concept of hierarchy is an abstraction which does not lend itself readily to dramatic enactment and has no ready-made mythology. Tragedy is reduced to private suffering, individual emotions, which have no social relevance.

It is possible that ultimately a socialist philosophy will become sufficiently established, with its own mythology, its own universally accepted taboos, for the tragic pattern to be re-established. I am not sure that I welcome the possibility of such a revival, since it would involve more than a recognition of the fact that no man is an island. In the absence of a belief in God, Society would have to be the new Divinity, and this is an absolutism which can be catastrophic. In the past the tragic pattern has been a way of justifying the ways of God to man. Evolving a tragic tradition in purely political terms would mean the development of a philosophy whereby the ends were seen to justify the means, a path with obvious pitfalls.

Perhaps we have reached a stage of evolution where we must accept, once and for all, that there is no reason for suffering, that pain and misery is arbitrary and not a punishment for wrong-doing. Perhaps we have left the world of the nursery and finally grown up.

Introduction
1 G. Murray, *Aeschylus* (1940), pp. 124–5.

Tribal Drama and Belief
1 S. Freud, *Totem and Taboo* (1913).
2 B. Spencer and F. Gillen, *Northern Tribes of Central Australia* (1904), p. 249.
3 *Ibid.*, pp. 179–82.
4 *Ibid.*, p. 182.
5 *Ibid.*, p. 525.
6 *Ibid.*, p. 530.
7 *Ibid.*, p. 22.
8 *Idem. Native Tribes of Central Australia* (1899), p. 57.

Kingship
1 E. E. Evans-Pritchard, *The Divine Kingship of the Shilluk of the Nilotic Sudan* (1948), pp. 33–4.
2 G. Glotz, *The Greek City* (1929).
3 G. Lienhardt, *Divinity and Experience: The Religion of the Dinka* (1961).
4 W. Ralegh, *Maxims of State* (*Works*, Vol. 8, 1829).
5 *Idem., The Cabinet-Council* (*Works*, Vol. 8, 1829).
6 *Idem., Maxims of State* (*Works*, Vol. 8, 1829).

The Dead
1 B. Spencer and F. Gillen, *Northern Tribes of Central Australia* (1904), pp. 518–29.
2 B. Malinowski, *Crime and Custom in Savage Society* (1926).
3 C. G. Seligman, *Pagan Tribes of the Nilotic Sudan* (1932).
4 J. Roscoe, *The Baganda* (1911), p. 98.
5 E. E. Evans-Pritchard, *Nuer Religion* (1956), p. 175.
6 L. Mair, *Primitive Government* (1964), pp. 179–80.
7 I. Schapera, *Government and Politics in Tribal Societies* (1956), p. 84.

Women
1 M. Meyer, *Henrik Ibsen*, Vol. 3 (1971), p. 146.
2 V. Turner, *The Ritual Process* (1969).

Order and Hierarchy
1 G. Glotz, *The Greek City* (1929).
2 A. Schlegel, *Lectures on Dramatic Art and Literature* (1808), Lecture 2.
3 B. Spencer and F. Gillen, *Northern Tribes of Central Australia* (1904), p. 32.
4 W. K. C. Guthrie, *The Greeks and their Gods* (1968), p. 184.

INDEX